Food, Culture & Society

an international journal of multidisciplinary research

vol 8 : number 2 :: *fall* 2005

BERG

Food, Culture & Society

Formerly *The Journal for the Study of Food and Society*

Aims and Scope

Food, Culture & Society is published by the Association for the Study of Food and Society (ASFS). ASFS is a multidisciplinary international organization dedicated to exploring the complex relationships among food, culture, and society. Its members approach the study of food from numerous disciplines in the humanities, social sciences, as well as in the world of food beyond the academy.

Striving to represent the highest standards of research and scholarship in all aspects of food studies, we encourage vigorous debate on a wide range of topics and problems, such as: cross-cultural perspectives on eating behaviors; gender and the food system; the food voice; recipes, cookbooks, and menus as texts; philosophical and religious perspectives on food and the body; social construction of culinary practices, beliefs, and traditions; politics of the family meal; dietary transitions; psychological, cultural, and social determinants of taste; methodological issues in food studies; malnutrition, hunger, and food security; commodity chain and foodshed analysis; food in fiction, film, and art; comparative food history; social and cultural dimensions of food technologies; political economy of the global food system; food studies pedagogy; plus original reviews of relevant books, films, videos, and exhibitions.

Editorial Board

Editor: Warren Belasco, *University of Maryland Baltimore County*

International Editor: Anne Murcott, *Special Professor, Nottingham University*

Book Review Editor: Ken Albala, *University of the Pacific*

Education Editor: Jonathan Deutsch, *Kingsborough Community College, CUNY*

International Advisory Board

Amy Bentley
New York University

Dorothy Blair
Pennsylvania State University

Jukka Gronow
Uppsala University

Annie Hubert
Centre National de la Recherche Scientifique (CNRS)

Alice Julier
Smith College

Rachel Laudan
Food historian, Guanajuato

Marianne Lien
University of Oslo

A. Lynn Martin
University of Adelaide

Alex McIntosh
Texas A&M University

Stephen Mennell
University College Dublin

Fabio Parasecoli
Gambero Rosso, Rome

Elaine Power
Queens University, Canada

Krishnendu Ray
New York University

Peter Scholliers
Vrije Universiteit Brussel

Andrew Smith
American Forum for Global Education

Jeffery Sobal
Cornell University

Rebecca Spang
University College London

Richard Wilk
Indiana University

Doris Witt
University of Iowa

Rafia Zafar
Washington University

ASFS Officers

President
Alice Julier
Smith College
ajulier@smith.edu

Vice President
Netta Davis
Boston University
netta_davis@harvard.edu

Treasurer and Membership
Jennifer Berg
New York University
jennifer.berg@nyu.edu

Secretary and Listserv Manager
Jonathan Deutsch
Kingsborough Community College, CUNY
jdeutsch@kbcc.cuny.edu

Journal Editor
Warren Belasco
University of Maryland Baltimore County
belasco@umbc.edu

Chair of Paper Prize Committee
Jacqueline Newman
Queens College, CUNY
Jloveschfd@aol.com

Newsletter Editor and Webmaster
Gary Allen
Independent Food Writer
gallen@hvi.net

Associate Newsletter Editor
Jeanne W. Lawless
Ithaca College
jlawless@ithaca.edu

Submissions

Authors do not have to be members of ASFS to submit articles. We prefer that contributors send their paper electronically via email to the editor, Warren Belasco: belasco@umbc.edu. Notes for Contributors can be found at the back of the journal.

Subscription Information

2005. Volume 8. 2 issues.
2006 onwards. Volume 9. 3 issues per year.
Free online subscription to institutional subscribers.
Electronic access through www.ingenta.com or www.ingentaconnect.com.

Subscription Rates

Institutional £100/$190
Individual £30/$55*
Student rate £160/$30*

*These prices are available only to personal subscribers and must be prepaid by personal cheque or credit card.

Ordering Options

Online: www.bergpublishers.com
By Email:
   custserv@turpin-distribution.com
By Mail: Berg Publishers
   c/o Turpin Distribution
   Stratton Business Park
   Pegasus Drive
   Biggleswade SG18 8TQ
   United Kingdom
By Phone: +44 (0)1767 604 951
By Fax: +44 (0)1767 601 604

Inquiries

Editorial: Kathryn Earle,
kearle@bergpublishers.com
Production: Ken Bruce,
kbruce@bergpublishers.com
Advertising and subscriptions:
Veruschka Selbach,
vselbach@bergpublishers.com

Reprints can be obtained from the publisher at the appropriate fees. Write to: Veruschka Selbach, Berg Publishers, 1st Floor, Angel Court, 81 St Clements Street, Oxford OX4 1AW, UK.

© 2005 Association for the Study of Food and Society. All rights reserved. No part of this publication may be reproduced, stored in a retrieval system, or transmitted in any form or by any means, including electronic, mechanical, photocopying, microfilming, recording, or otherwise (except for that copying permitted by Sections 107 and 108 of the US Copyright Law and except by reviewers for the public press) without written permission from the Association. More information about ASFS may be found at: http://food-culture.org/

ISSN: 1552-8014

Published by Berg Publishers on behalf of ASFS. Berg Publishers is the imprint of Oxford International Publishers Ltd.

Cover and text based on designs by Guenet Abraham
Typeset by Avocet Typeset, Chilton, Aylesbury, Bucks
Printed in the UK

Contents : :

141 *From the Editor*

Articles

143 "How Unripe We Are": The Intellectual Construction of American Foodways
JAMES E. McWILLIAMS

161 In the Absence of Food: A Case of Rhythmic Loss and Spoiled Identity for Patients with Percutaneous Endoscopic Gastrostomy Feeding Tubes
ASHBY WALKER

181 "Beef. It's What's for Dinner": Vegetarians, Meat-Eaters and the Negotiation of Familial Relationships
LUANNE K. ROTH

201 Food, Feelings and Film: Women's Power in *Like Water for Chocolate*
CAROLE COUNIHAN

215 Home to McDonald's: Upholding the Family Dinner with the Help of McDonald's
HELENE BREMBECK

Commentary

227 The Pleasure of Diversity in Slow Food's Ethics of Taste
KELLY DONATI

Perspectives on Teaching

243 Literary Approaches to Food Studies: Eating the Other
KYLA WAZANA TOMPKINS

Book Reviews

259 Jessamyn Neuhaus, *Manly Meals and Mom's Home Cooking: Cookbooks and Gender in Modern America*, reviewed by Alice McLean

Theodore C. Bestor, *Tsukiji: The Fish Market at the Center of the World*, reviewed by Michael Ashkenazi

Margaret McWilliams, *Foods: Experimental Perspectives, Fifth Edition*, and *Experimental Foods: Laboratory Manual, Sixth Edition*, reviewed by Jeffrey Miller.

Julie Guthman, *Agrarian Dreams: The Paradox of Organic Farming in California*, reviewed by Janet Chrzan

269 Contributors

271 Notes for Contributors

From the Editor : :

This issue offers a wealth of insights into the complex—and often contentious—ways in which we use food to construct national, family, and personal identities. Food historians have long been debating whether there is a distinctly "American" cuisine, and in "How Unripe We Are," James E. McWilliams shows how the attempt to distinguish frontier "rusticity and practicality" from Old World "luxury, sloth, and indulgence" dates back at least as far as the Revolutionary era. If food has a major role in giving voice to nationalist political aspirations, the next four articles demonstrate its power as an expression of everyday family politics. Ashby Walker's award-winning essay on Percutaneous Endoscopic Gastrostomy (PEG) feeding tubes examines what happens to personal identity and family dynamics when people lose the ability to eat. Along similar lines, LuAnne Roth's ironically titled "Beef. It's What's for Dinner," looks at the major challenges posed for family meal rituals when a member "becomes vegetarian." On a more affirmative note, Carole Counihan uses the classic film *Like Water for Chocolate* to explore the surprisingly subversive ways in which women can exercise power through cooking. If Counihan's analysis supports the idea that the traditional kitchen can be a site of empowerment rather than enslavement, Helene Brembeck's study of how Swedish families use McDonald's takes us in a rather different direction, as she contests the popular assumption that fast food is a threat to the vitality of "the home." For the Slow Food movement, of course, fast food *is* the enemy, and in a continuation of a discussion that we started in the Fall 2004 issue of FCS (vol. 7, issue 2), Kelly Donati suggests a possible theoretical reconciliation between Slow Food's subversive and elitist tendencies. Then, as part of our ongoing series on food pedagogy, Kyla Wazana Tompkins shows how she incorporates many of these themes into a dynamic undergraduate course titled "Eating the Other."

Warren Belasco

EDUCATE YOUR *palate*

Turn your love of food into a graduate education—

THE MASTER OF LIBERAL ARTS IN **GASTRONOMY** AT **BOSTON UNIVERSITY**

Since 1991, the gastronomy program has been examining the role of food from a multidisciplinary perspective encompassing the arts and humanities as well as the natural and social sciences.

Study history, geography, nutrition, sociology, art, literature, cuisine, anthropology ... all with a central focus on food and its integral place in world culture.

Design a curriculum that matches your interests— the full breadth of Boston University's world-class faculty and academic departments are at your fingertips.

You can choose to study part- or full-time.

OTHER CULINARY **AND** GASTRONOMY **PROGRAMS AT** BOSTON UNIVERSITY:

- 14-Week Certificate in the Culinary Arts
- Wine Studies
- Cheese Certificate
- Wine and Food Seminars

www.bu.edu/met/mla | 617-353-9852 | gastrmla@bu.edu

James E. **McWilliams**
Texas State University

·."How Unripe We Are"

THE INTELLECTUAL CONSTRUCTION OF
AMERICAN FOODWAYS

This article demonstrates the political and cultural consequences of food production as they played out during the Revolutionary era. The Seven Years' War and the Revolutionary War itself demonstrated that access to food was inseparable from access to freedom. After delineating this political education, the article goes on to show how Americans drew heavily on a specific intellectual construction of food in order to distinguish themselves from what they were coming to condemn as European luxury, sloth, and indulgence. In the process, their constructions—if European accounts are to be believed—gradually came to fruition as Americans began to highlight the virtues of a "frontier" style of cooking and eating that emphasized rusticity and practicality.

: :

"No taxation without representation!" went the preferred rallying cry of revolutionary Americans. The phrase effectively captured the constitutional principles that the mother country repeatedly violated throughout the 1760s and early 1770s. It forcefully reminds us that disgruntled Americans decided to fight a revolution based in part on their realization that the otherwise beloved mother country was abridging English liberties dating back to the Glorious Revolution. At the same time, however, this highly politicized plea reflected much more. While stressing the overtly political nature of colonial discontent, the mantra illuminated the important but less obvious reality that the items being taxed were often directly related to the colonists' ability to produce and trade local goods without interference. Common patriots responded as much to the emotional appeal of political abstractions as they did to the concrete reality of material life. Perhaps the point is too obvious to state, but nothing was more central to material life than the production and consumption of food. This usually vague—and always unarticulated—connection among food, local trade, and revolutionary activity assumed pointed political implications during the Revolutionary era for a very simple reason: if there was one customary right that white colonists throughout the colonies instinctively understood it was their ability to produce and consume the literal fruits of their labor. To study the Revolutionary era without appreciating this connection is to miss how Americans relied on food during an especially fragile period not only to feed themselves, but to do nothing less than define who they were.

In the colonial context, America's self-reliance in food production was exactly how it should have been. England hardly wanted to waste time and money supplying its most peripheral colonies with foodstuffs. Instead, it urged the colonies to become self-sufficient with respect to food and, in turn, dependent on England for manufactured goods. Throughout their short history, the colonists dutifully met these goals, sustaining the transatlantic symbiosis while producing an abundance and plethora of food products, trading them amongst themselves, and protesting none at all when Britain discouraged their nascent manufacturing schemes. At the same time, though, what the colonies had gone through to achieve such self-sufficiency—clearing land, planting fields, raising cattle, establishing networks of trade—made them rightfully (even defensively) proud of how well they had fulfilled their side of the bargain. Free colonies had taken hoe to hard dirt and built farms to feed their families and had produced an impressive surplus to sell in regional markets. It was no mean feat. These regional markets, in turn, slowly expanded, the rum trade pulled the colonial regions together through the tangible charms of sugar, molasses, and intoxication, and the major colonial areas wove themselves into the transatlantic economy through cod, wheat, tobacco and rice. These productions were more than mere commodities. Indeed, they were symbolic reflections of the ceaseless toil that Americans and their slaves, servants, and children invested in the ongoing quest for self-sufficiency. As these economic developments transpired, the average free white colonist came to enjoy something that his ancestors only dreamed of enjoying: access to a wide range of foodstuffs. Preserving that privilege was a cultural imperative that few talked about. Nobody, however, took it for granted.[1]

The relatively unfettered ability to acquire food was a notable reflection of the colonies' impressive economic growth. The colonial economy expanded by an average annual rate of 3.5% between 1650 and 1770. It was an especially remarkable accomplishment considering the *English* standard—a mere 0.5% over the same time period. Per capita income in America rose from $572 to $1,043, or 0.49% a year. While the slave-produced exports of sugar, rice, and tobacco accounted for much of this growth and income, the vast majority of the food produced in colonial America—perhaps as much as 85%—was consumed *in colonial America*.[2] The colonists had succeeded in building a dynamic internal economy in the long cast of the empire's shadow. It was an economy, moreover, that offered immigrants to America a better chance of living in relative material ease and comfort. "That the colonists were able to produce significant food surpluses despite the consumption trends of a rapidly growing population," writes David Klingaman, "is one reason for believing, as most economic historians do, that substantial extensive growth was taking place."[3] The fact that the colonial American population expanded from 1.5 million to 2.5 million between 1754 and 1775, not to mention that the colonies' standard of living was on the rise and very few white families wanted for food, spoke powerfully to the reality of America's crucial transition to material security.

The colonies performed especially well with respect to food production and internal trade from 1768 until 1772. Provincial regions specialized to the extent that they were soon producing and systematically exporting goods to each other. Webs of regional dependency evolved. Connecticut, New York, New Jersey, Pennsylvania, Delaware, Maryland, Virginia, and North Carolina supplied bread and flour to Maine, New Hampshire, Massachusetts, Rhode Island, South Carolina, and Georgia. Connecticut, Maryland, Virginia, and Pennsylvania supplied Massachusetts, Rhode, Island, Delaware, and New Jersey with wheat. Corn came to all the New England colonies from every middle and southern colony. Georgia, the Carolinas, Rhode Island, Virginia, Delaware, Pennsylvania, and Connecticut produced beef and pork for Maine, New Hampshire, Massachusetts, New Jersey, and Maryland.[4] These connections pulled together the once isolated regional trends that characterized eating habits throughout the colonies while fostering a more varied diet for a population whose nutritional needs remained, on the labor intensive colonial periphery, especially substantial. Americans—even as they engaged in considerable overseas exportation—were producing more food then they could consume and they were sharing it with impressive regularity. This accomplishment was worth guarding.

When England thus decided to tighten its grasp on the colonies after the Seven Years' War through legislative measures that affected food-related items, it touched sensitive nerves. In 1764 came the Sugar Act. This act built on the Molasses Act of 1733, which aimed to provide the British sugar growers a monopoly on the mainland market by imposing a tax on the sugar, molasses, and rum imported from the French and Dutch West Indies. Smuggling by American merchants soon rendered the act a dead letter. But now, thirty-one years later, England decided to pass the Sugar Act as a way to enforce the preexisting duty on sugar and reimpose its monopoly on the sugar trade within the colonies. The Quartering Act followed in 1765, subjecting the entirety of colonial farm produce to random seizures. Indeed, the Quartering Act specifically required colonial authorities to provide food, drink, quarters, and fuel to the redcoats stationed in their villages. The Townshend Duties came after the 1765 Stamp Act, placing a duty on many manufactured imports and luxury goods, including tea. The duties also leveled severe restrictions on the colonists' ability to trade both at home and abroad by imposing arbitrary customs collections. More insultingly, revenue from customs duties was earmarked to finance even more customs officials, spies, searches and seizures, writs of assistants, and the establishment of a Board of Customs Commissioners in Boston—all of which curtailed the brisk and systematic trade in food and other goods that the colonists had been nurturing for decades. These measures tampered with the colonies' food supply and, in so doing, helped inspire a simmering political response.[5]

Acts passed in the 1770s brought the situation to a boil. In 1770, the imperial relationship initially looked like it was on the mend. The Crown repealed the Townshend Duties on every product except—just to reiterate its authority—tea. Still, three years of relative peace prevailed because the colonists, who had developed an intense love of tea during the British invasion, were able to buy it from the ever-resourceful Dutch smugglers. But the Tea Act, passed in 1773, undermined this customary arrangement. Designed to offload 17 million pounds of tea that bulged in the ailing East India Company's warehouses, the Tea Act rearranged excise regulations to allow the company to pay the Townshend duty on tea while still undercutting competitors. In essence, Lord North and his ministry were imposing a direct tax on the colonists while forcing them—if they continued to drink tea—to bail out the East India Company. The response was the Boston Tea Party. In December of 1773, a group of patriots dressed as Mohawk Indians ceremoniously dumped 342 chests of East India tea into Boston Harbor with the approval of a cheering crowd. The act provoked Lord North to impose the Boston Port Act, effectively isolating Boston from the rest of the trading world until Massachusetts paid for the destroyed tea. At this point, the rhetoric of discontent intensified. Fifteen months later, about twenty miles from where the tea was dumped, it exploded into rebellion.

As historians have long noted, war erupted because the offensive measures—the Sugar Act, Tea Act, the Quartering Act, the Stamp Act, the Townshend Duties, the Coercive Acts—corrupted the basic liberties that white colonists assumed as members of the British Empire. At the same time that these policies trod on the white colonists' natural rights, however, they also challenged their customary access to material goods—including foodstuff such as sugar, tea, and a wide variety of farm produce. These items meant more than sweetness, bitterness, and hearty fare. The consumption of food and drink had become, by the 1760s, vivid manifestations of several cultural values—values deeply entwined with the concept of "liberty." They represented concrete aspects of life such as the colonists' upward mobility, their increasing freedom of choice, and even their dignity as British Americans. The widespread acquisition of not only food and drink themselves, but also their visible accoutrements—tea kettles, tea chests, china, tankards, bowls, plates, and many other manufactured baubles—also became powerful psychological expressions for many white colonial Americans. These goods provided the language and grammar of daily life, the markers of rank, the sweet rewards of persistence. They were, as a result, integral to the larger sense of liberty that colonists believed was sacred enough to fight the American Revolution to protect. And thus, upon this logic, British Americans evolved into reluctant revolutionaries.[6]

The tendency to interpret political infringements through food saw its most radical expression in over thirty local food riots that flared up between 1775 and 1779. Whereas the Empire's onerous policies had interrupted the free trade in goods that colonists had come to take for granted, the Revolutionary War erected obstacles even more daunting. The resulting scarcity of both locally produced and imported food from the West Indies—

which did not join the rebellion—motivated many merchants to succumb to the seductive temptation of price gouging their compatriots. American consumers, however, reacted with defensiveness reminiscent of the kind they had honed in the decade before the war. As Barbara Smith explains, "rioters and their allies claimed that confronting merchants in their shops was a patriotic action, much like facing redcoats on the battlefield."[7] In the process, the defense of food provided an accessible political education that buttressed the larger and more conspicuous defense of freedom.

The connection between political agitation and food supply, as Smith shows, became manifestly evident in several well-documented incidents. In July 1776, a group from Longmeadow, Massachusetts, blackened their faces, wrapped themselves in blankets, and told Jonathan Hale, a Tory merchant, about their "uneasiness with those that trade in rum, molasses, and sugar." They explained, "it is a matter of great grief that you Should give us cause to call upon you in this uncommon way ... We find you guilty of very wrong behaviour in selling at extravagant prices." The crowd looked forward to "a Thorough reformation for time to come," and proffered a list of acceptable prices. Hale dutifully complied. After the crowd finished with Hale they paid a visit to Samuel Colton, another Longmeadow merchant of dubious loyalty whose prices were deemed "detrimental to the Liberties of America." Colton, however, was a bit more stubborn. He refused to lower the cost of his goods, leading the crowd to confiscate his imports and hide them in a nearby barn. Duly chastised, Colton "made prayer in publick" and lowered his prices. A week later, however, he raised them again. This time the crowd, having dispensed with "moderate measures," confiscated his goods and destroyed his store. They "ransacked [the warehouse] from top to bottom," Colton testified, causing him "great Fear and Terr'r." The goods were hauled over to the town clerk, who sold them at the requested rates. The profits were later offered to Colton, who spitefully refused them. Undeterred, the crowd simply dropped the cash at his house and left.[8]

In New York a month later the issue was tea, the rioters a group of women, and the recalcitrant merchant Jacobus Lefferts. Lefferts refused to sell his tea at 6s/lb, as the Continental Congress suggested. Pushing his tea at 9s/lb, a rate that the local paper said was designed "to make a prey of the friends of the US by asking the most exorbitant price," he ignored a "committee of ladies" who were protesting in front of store. He did so, however, at his own peril, for they eventually seized the tea, appointed a clerk, parceled the tea into 6s/lb amounts, and sold them to local inhabitants. Jefferts, however, wasn't fortunate enough to have the proceeds dumped on his doorstep. Instead, the committee sent them to the Revolutionary county committee, which dispersed the funds to support the war effort.[9]

These events were relatively commonplace because access to food and food-related goods was integral to the most basic material values that

Americans had embraced over the course of their short but steady history of economic growth. When seventeen men from Maryland seized salt from an unscrupulous merchant, when a "quarrel for bread" erupted at a Massachusetts bakery, when New York crowds seized food wagons, when sixty women confiscated sugar in Beverly, Massachusetts, when Bostonians forced a French baker to make the town bread, when Virginians announced "measures by the MOB" would keep prices down, or when Philadelphians armed with clubs bullied shopkeepers to behave fairly, rebellious Americans—especially women—reiterated the popular assumption that political ideology and action responded to Americans' rightful access to their own food supply. "The very honey of our bees," John Hector St. Jean Crevecoeur later observed about the American farm, "comes from this privileged spot."[10] Food, as Crevecoeur well knew, was worth a good fight.

The Deeper Roots of American Food Fights

The revolutionary relationship between food and political freedom did not emerge spontaneously. It had its immediate roots in the Seven Years' War. This war, which actually lasted nine years (1754–63), placed France, Austria, Saxony, Sweden, and Russia against Great Britain, Prussia, and Hanover. The North American theater saw Britain and France battling for the vast colonial territory ranging from the Atlantic to the Mississippi. The fight began over ownership of the Upper Ohio River Valley and from that scrape intensified into a fight over whose empire the sun would never set upon. England, whose resources were stretched to the breaking point, relied heavily on the colonies not only for military support but also for food.[11] And that's the issue upon which brewing internal disagreements hinged.

Much as the colonists' behavior during and just after the Revolution suggests, they were none too eager to part ways with their hard-earned access to material goods, even for their own soldiers and the British regiments fighting the French. A typical weekly food allowance for a British soldier during the war included seven pounds of beef, four pounds of pork, seven pounds of bread, three pints of peas or beans, a half-pound of rice, and a quarter pound of butter. Parliament attempted to contract with colonial governments to supply these rations, but more often than not, what the soldiers ended up with was scurvy, an ailment resulting from a lack of fresh meat and vegetables. Fresh garden produce, recently milled flour, and freshly slaughtered meat were rarely and reluctantly forthcoming from American farmers more intent on supplying their own needs and trading surpluses locally than making contributions to a distant military cause. Soldiers were routinely left to eat hard salted pork and stale bread without vegetables. In 1759, the men of the 42nd regimen sat down to a dinner of "ship's beef" and bacon "which had been in store since the former war and Biscuits full of maggots, so that after endeavoring to clear them of vermin we used to wet them and toast them."[12] The Deputy Commissary of Stores surveyed the troops' food inventory before a 1758 expedition and lamented how they had to set out with "mouldy Bisket," "rusty salt pork" that was "extream bad" with much of it being "rotten and stunk." From Lake George in 1758, Joseph Nicols remarked how "Our army is very much uneasy with their manner of living. Our allowance at present is only flour and pork ... we labor under a great disadvantage." It was not a condition easily tolerated in a land producing a surplus of foodstuffs.

The lack of food supplies began to take its toll in terms of military performance. To prepare General Braddock for his campaign against the French at Niagara and Crown Point, the army arranged to acquire food from suppliers in New York, Rhode Island, Connecticut, Virginia, and Maryland. The Governor of Rhode Island tried to rouse his colonists with a pep talk, explaining, "Hence every Government, concerned in the present Enterprise will, I doubt not, proportion supplies according to the value they put upon their religion, their liberty, their estates, and the freedom of themselves and their posterity." He should have had his doubts. New York failed to supply beef. Albany merchants refused to accept notes from other colonies for peas and bread. Maryland and Virginia delivered rations so damaged that Braddock erupted, "They had promised everything and performed nothing!" Virginia would only release provisions if they were earmarked for Virginians. Pennsylvania farmers complained about having to travel long distances to exchange farm produce for cash, leading many to renege on their promised deliveries. Braddock's regimen was soon reduced to half rations, then a quarter. When the Massachusetts Governor tried to impress horses and wagons from local farmers to make an emergency delivery of food, the farmers refused violently. As Braddock moved towards his target, his men were on the brink of mutiny; while he pulled though in the end, it was in spite of the food supply. The British, described by one observer as "a poor pitiful handful of half starved, scorbutic skeletons," only defeated the French at the Battle of Sainte-Foy because the French, too, were "melted down to Three Thousand fighting men, most by Inveterate Scurvy."[13]

The widespread intransigence on the part of American farmers to provide food for British soldiers was often met with responses that motivated them to hoard their food supply even more selfishly. Soldiers descended on local farms to steal apples from orchards, pigs from pens, and cattle from meadows. British soldiers combed over so many New York farms that Albany, which repeatedly noted robberies of "sheep Fowl & Roots of all kinds carried off in the Night," had to post guards around targeted settlements and fine soldiers wondering off camp after dark. Much to his chagrin, General Gage spent considerable time responding to complaints that his troops had plundered local gardens and orchards, often at gun point. His task was made no easier by the fact that many Generals sanctioned these raids, as Amherst did when his troops picked clean a Massachusetts orchard.[14]

Farmers did not react kindly to this behavior. In fact, they responded to raids by practicing the time-honored techniques of price gouging and bilking what they could from the government trough. When demand for food spiked among British regiments, so did its price. Peas that had been selling for 5s suddenly jumped to 6s. Bread rose 2s per hundredweight when soldiers knocked. As one historian explains, "the lure of war profiteering was greater than patriotism."[15] Profiteering was especially rampant after the crown officially took over the financing of supplies in 1756. Trusting the predictable laxity in government oversight, colonial governments filed receipts and were often compensated for goods that had nothing to do with war supplies. Rhode Island, for example, managed to get the Crown to foot the bill for a merchant's shipment of coffee, tea, chocolate, sugar, ham, knives, forks, spoons, and plates—none of which made it to the British soldiers, going instead into Rhode Island homes.

To a very large extent, the intolerable policies that violated American freedom from 1763 to 1775 were, in addition to impolitic revenue-generating policies, expressions of anger toward the colonists for their wartime antics. A paradox of the Seven Years' War was thus that, in eliminating the French threat to North American land and security, the British found themselves at odds with their own colonies. On the one hand, the colonies experienced a surge in British loyalty after the war. They were proud to be part of an Empire that single-handedly controlled North America; they were eager to work with England through the pursuit of economic self-interest through transatlantic and inter-coastal trade. On the other hand, though, the English were irate at the arrogance of their colonial subjects. In addition to providing less than impressive supplies, the colonists took advantage of the war to violate trade laws that stretched back to 1651, traded with the enemy when it was convenient to do so, and generally convinced England that it was high time to bring them down a notch or two.[16] Hence the Sugar Act, the Quartering Act, the Stamp Act, the Tea Act—all retaliations in one way or another at least indirectly related to food, an item which was, not coincidentally, a major point of contention during the Seven Years' War. Historians have described this sudden flip-flop on the part of Parliament and the Crown as a gross violation of customary relationships. As the events before and after the Revolution suggest, however, it was also a violation of the very item that shaped the colonists' social and economic life: their food. None of this is to say that violations of food *caused* the Revolution. But they certainly were a factor.

The Cultivation of a Pastoral Ideal after the Revolution

Much as food contextualized colonial behavior before and during the American Revolution, it played an influential role in redefining American culture in the Revolution's aftermath. In the larger effort of the US to shed all remnants of English culture, Americans embraced the rough edges of American foodways to foster a pastoral ideal that promoted the frontier values that the colonists had once downplayed. Indeed, whereas Americans once worked to overcome the hayseed associations of the periphery, striving instead for sophisticated metropolitan ideals, they now highlighted their relative lack of cultivation—a trait best reflected not so much in the food itself but in the work that accounted for it: farming. The virtue of the frontier and farming became especially clear to proponents of what was then known as the conjectural theory of history. According to this theory, being associated with agricultural life meant being far away from the debilitating threshold of commercialism, a threshold that England had so recently passed. Noah Webster grasped the advantages of the frontier and its promise of continued agricultural nourishment when he characterized the evolution away from agriculture as "a period that every benevolent man will deprecate and endeavor to retard."[17] By adhering to the pull of a frontier that the Seven Years' War had effectively cleared of Indians, America would not be "hurried down the stream of corruption with other nations." Whereas "In the United States everything that has been done hitherto in the construction of cities is an imitation of the old European ... mode," an idealized version of the agrarian life would show, by contrast, that the old way "of course is *wrong*."[18]

Farmers might have believed this idea intuitively, but influential Americans made it a matter of public discourse. Americans could and very much did promote the idea that—as Franklin phrased it—"*Commerce* ... is generally *Cheating*" while farming "is the only *honest Way* ... to acquire wealth."[19] Whereas the frontier, according to Crevecoeur, once represented the nation's "feeble beginnings and barbarous rudiments," it now became the raw material necessary for an "industrious people" to transform into "fine, fertile, well regulated" farms. A "hundred years ago," Crevecoeur continued, the colonies were "wild, wooly, and uncultivated." Now they comprised an "immense country" marked by "substantial villages, extensive fields ... decent houses, good roads, orchards, meadows, and bridges."[20] Thus, the colonists went from "barbarous" beginnings to a polished culture through the singular and ongoing act of farming, an act that combined frontier values with nation's food supply in way that distinguished America from its English agrarian tradition.

Perhaps no prominent American enthusiastically sang the praises of the unique frontier and the agricultural life it fostered more than Thomas

Jefferson. His oft-quoted pronouncements on the pastoral ideal have become America's secular scripture. "Those who labour in the earth," he wrote, "are the chosen people of God." England had succumbed to degenerate behavior as it embraced manufacturing, but America was—for the time being at least—safe from such a fate because, as Jefferson noticed, "[c]orruption of morals in the mass of cultivators is a phenomenon of which no age nor nation has furnished an example." America was truly exceptional in that it could realistically wish "never ... to see our citizens occupied at a workbench, or twirling a distaff."[21] Those who worked in shops, as England's recent history had shown, bred corruption and made life unnecessarily complicated. Such a turn of events for England was to be expected, Jefferson continued, because dependence on other nations for something as basic as food "suffocates the germ of virtue, and prepares fit tools for the designs of ambition." Although he had a tendency to contradict himself with disarming consistency, Jefferson doled out this advice consistently.

Jefferson and others like him considered the virtues of husbandry to be seductive enough—if properly popularized—to hold the nation together after the American Revolution. The strongest thread running through the varied tapestry of American farming, however, was a related notion integral to the frontier and the food it produced: simplicity. Jefferson implored the young American man to avoid Europe because, once there, "[h]e acquires a fondness for European luxury and dissipation and a contempt for the simplicity of his own country." The simplicity of the farming life enchanted Crevecoeur as well. After thanking God "that my lot is to be an American farmer," he explained the virtues of his chosen profession. There was the generational connection to his father, who "left me a good farm, and his experience; he left me free from debts, and no kind of difficulties to struggle with." When it came to his food supply, the farming life was beyond repute. Crevecoeur remarked, "Every year I kill from 1,500 to 2,000 weight of pork, 1,200 of beef, half a dozen of good wethers in harvest; of fowls my wife has always a great stock: what can I wish more"? Merely walking onto his farm sent him into rapture. "The instant I enter on my own land, the bright idea of property, of exclusive right, of independence exalt my mind. Precious soil, I say to myself ... what should we American farmers be without the distinct possession of that soil? It feeds, it clothes us, from it we draw even a great exuberancy, our best meat, our richest drink."[22] Richard Price, a Unitarian minister from Virginia, spoke equally approvingly of "an independent and hardy YEOMANRY, all nearly on a level ... clothed in homespun—of simple manners—strangers to luxury—drawing plenty from the ground—and that plenty, gathered easily by the hand of industry."[23] The frontier and the food that yeoman produced on it thus became emblematic of the simple virtues that Americans, if only rhetorically, used to define and direct their young nation.

With respect to food, Americans would thus enjoin the values of the Revolution with their varied culinary pasts in order to create an "American" food that would find its counterpart nowhere else in the world. American food not only inspired the American cultural ideal of rugged simplicity undisturbed by the magnetic pull of metropolitan sophistication. At the same time, the frontier and its simple connotations turned around to shape American food into an explicitly recognizable culinary style that Americans wore as a badge of honor, no matter how often the Europeans turned up their noses.

Cookbooks and the Evolution of Culinary Rusticity
::

The agrarian values that colonists fought the Revolution to preserve became the same values that Americans would use to instill their new food ways with even earthier connotations than they had during the colonial era. A telling example of how Americans thought about their food in the wake of political independence comes from the early American dramatist William Dunlap, who promoted his play *The Father* as "a frugal plain repast," contrasting it to the "high seasoned food" dished out by European dramatists.[24] Without in any way intending to, Dunlap points us in the direction of the intellectual origins of American food.

Like their newly articulated political principles, Americans wanted their food to be free of affectation. The cookbooks published in early America were largely reflections of the English system of cookery that more often than not plagiarized old English sources rather than recording American innovations. Nevertheless, a sense of America's culinary "return to homespun" comes through in several recipes. Selections from American cookbooks after 1796 (when the first one was published) often use ingredients native to America in their recipes. Amelia Simmons' *American Cookery* basically lifted English recipes from Richard Briggs' *The New Art of Cookery*. Nevertheless, it still published such recipes as "cramberry sauce," "pompkin pie," Indian pudding, and cornmeal bread.[25] Hannah Glasse's *The Art of Cookery Made Plain and Easy*, published in Virginia in 1805, also reads like an old English cookbook, with the exception of seven wonderful pages, all included under the subtitle "several new receipts adapted to the American mode of cooking."[26] These recipes stand out in stark contrast to the rest of the book for their pared down simplicity. A brief sampling conveys a taste of this "American mode" while providing a telling point of comparison to European traditions.

> To Make Pumpkin Pie
> Take the Pumpkin and peel the rind off, then stew it till it is quite soft, and put thereto one pint of pumpkin, one pint of milk, one glass

of Malaga wine, one glass of rose-water, if you like it, seven eggs, half a pound of fresh butter, one small nutmeg, and sugar and salt to your taste.

To Make Blood Puddings

Take your Indian meal ... and scald it with boiled milk or water, then stir in your blood, straining it first, mince the hog's lard and put it in the pudding, then season it with treacle ... put it in a bag and let it boil six or seven hours.

To Make Peach Sweetmeats

To one pound of Peaches put half a pound of good brown sugar, with a half a pint of water to dissolve it, first clarifying it with an egg; then boil the peaches and sugar together, skimming the egg off ... till it is of the thickness of a jelly ... pears are done the same way.

These recipes are unusual in that they were meant to be followed by most American cooks. Unlike the more traditional English recipes published in Glasse's book, they generally incorporate native ingredients, or at least ingredients commonly available throughout America; they are described in a much more basic manner than English recipes and they are much easier recipes to execute than other recipes detailed in the book. The comparison of American pot-pie with the English mince pie reveals an obvious attempt to reduce the steps involved and the ingredients used. Her recipe for a traditional English mince pie is about four times as long and doubly involved. She calls for raisons, currants "picked, washed, rubbed, and dried at the fire," "half a hundred pippins pared, cored, and chopped small," sugar that is "pounded fine," cloves, nutmegs, and mace "all beat fine," layerings with Seville oranges, lemons, and the addition of a parboiled tongue for added flavor.[27] The simplicity of the American recipe quoted above becomes especially obvious when compared to the English recipe for "Cheshire Pork Pie." In this version, Glasse advised the cook to use a *loin* of pork rather than any old cut, to "lay a layer of pork, then a larger layer, of pippins, pared, cored and a little sugar ... then another layer of pork," and finally, a half pint of white wine.[28]

The simplified methods characterizing the "American mode" are further evident in a comparison of Glasse's American and English eel pie recipes. The "American mode" asked the cook to "skin your eels and parboil them, then season them with pepper and salt, and put them into your paste, with a half dozen raw oysters, one quarter of a pound of butter, and water." Instead of simply skinning and parboiling eels, by contrast, the English version demanded that the chef "clean, gut, and wash your eels very well, then cut them into pieces half as long as your finger." It also suggested the addition of "a little beaten mace to your palate." A comparison of how to make sausages reveals an English recipe that insists that the "skin and gristles" be removed and the guts "very nicely cleaned."[29] Significantly, the American version skips these procedures.

The implication couldn't have been any starker to American cooks: the "American mode" had no time and felt no need to remove the guts from eels, cut them into uniform pieces, and pamper the palette with a dusting of hand-milled mace. It saw no need to scrape gristles and skin from a pig before rendering it into sausage. Perhaps it would have back in 1750, when Americans were in awe of the British. But not in 1805, when Americans were in awe of themselves and their emerging rustic culture. The nature of a "frugal plain repast," after all, allowed none such frivolity.

The European Recognition of American Cuisine
: :

Through a purposeful embrace of culinary simplicity after the Revolution, Americans ate familiar foods under the increasingly popular assumption that eating was a practical rather than a ceremonial activity. Just as American culture had become more pragmatic, so had its food. When the British Foreign Minister visited the Secretary of State James Madison in 1777, he spoke volumes about the emerging distinctiveness of American food when he described Dolly's meal as "more like a harvest home supper than the entertainment of the Secretary of State." Dolly, upon hearing of this remark, retorted, "the profusion of my table arises from the happy circumstances and abundance and prosperity in our country."[30]

While Americans might have been only vaguely aware of the culinary transition occurring in their midst, their European contemporaries saw it more clearly. In 1804, a Frenchman visiting the United States was struck by the almost proud lack of refinement that characterized supposedly sophisticated meals. "They swallow," he wrote of his American hosts, "almost without chewing." The rusticity of the food thoroughly underwhelmed him. The Americans he visited ate "hot bread, half-baked, toast soaked in butter, cheese of the fattest kind, slices of salt or hung beef, ham, etc., all of which is nearly insoluble." Fearing that he might sound inhospitable, the Frenchman could not help but express his opinions that "at dinner they have boiled pastes under the name puddings, and their sauces, even for roast beef, are melted butter; their turnips and potatoes swim in hog's lard, butter, or fat; under the name of pie or pumpkin, their pastry is nothing but a greasy paste, never sufficiently baked."[31] What makes these comments even more revealing about the comparatively rustic nature of American food is the fact that this Frenchman was Constantin Francois de Chasseboeuf, Count of Volney. With a name and title like that we can be assured that he was not having his snobbish taste buds assaulted in backcountry taverns.

While the tendency might be to dismiss the Frenchman's opinion as exceptionally snotty, he was not alone. Twenty-five years later Harriet Martineau, an English visitor and the future author of *Society in America* (1837), graciously referred to America as a place where "sweet temper diffused like sunshine over the land." Evidently not, however, over its food. At best, she thought it quaint that Americans relied so heavily on simple fare for their sustenance. She repeatedly noted the popularity of cornbread, buckwheat cakes, eggs and bacon, broiled chicken, hominy, beefsteak, and pickled fish. The ubiquity of corn especially astounded her. "A man who has corn," she wrote, may have everything." In Virginia, however, she found all the food that she ate—mainly bread, butter, and coffee—to be stale. Her hosts' attitudes were evidently not much fresher. "They probably have no idea that there is better food than they set before us," she sneered. A search for mutton turned up nothing, and when Martineau moved from the East Coast to Tennessee, her culinary quest turned up a particularly horrible gustatory scrap. "The dish from which I ate," she recalled after one especially enigmatic meal, "was, according to some, mutton; to others, pork." "My own idea," she concluded, "was that it was dog."[32]

Even in Tennessee, however, they were not eating dogs. What Martineau failed to understand was that she was visiting a nation that had rejected European culinary habits and forged its own. Americans were perfectly at ease with unrefined, unpretentious food. Other foreigners visiting America better recognized this defining trait. Frederick Marryat, an Englishman, observed the offerings at a Broadway market and remarked tellingly on the lack of variety. "Broadway being three miles long," he explained, "and the booths lining each side of it, in every booth there was a roast pig, large or small, as the center of attraction. Six miles of roast pig!"[33] The Duke of Liancourt noted the Americans' seeming contentment with the most simple, monotonous diet. "Indian corn," he wrote, "was the national crop, and Indian corn was eaten three times a day" in addition to salt pork. "In the country," he continued, "fresh meat could not regularly be got, except in the shape of poultry or game; but the hog cost nothing to keep, and very little to kill and preserve. Thus the ordinary American was brought up on salt pork and Indian corn, or rye." Not that Americans had a problem with this fare. Thomas Ashe, writing in *Travels in America in 1806*, noted how many Americans preferred salted meat, recalling one timber worker who explained, "your fresh meat, that's too fancy ... and hain't got strength unto it." Charles Dickens confirmed the pragmatism behind American food when he noted a steady stream of "tea, coffee, bread, butter, salmon, shad, liver, steak, potatoes, pickles, ham, chops, black-puddings, and sausages," explaining how "dinner was breakfast again without the tea and coffee; and supper and breakfast were identical." In *The American Frugal Housewife* (1838), Lydia Maria Child offered advice that might be seen as the essence of early American food: "Nothing should be thrown away as long as it is possible to make use of it, however trifling that use may be."[34] The men, women, and children moving toward the Mississippi River, and taking with them their newly forged culinary values, would have well appreciated the suggestion.

Conclusion

As Americans who came of age during the Revolutionary era knew better than the historians who have studied them, food didn't exist in a vacuum. Food, in fact, was integral to the era's defining cultural and political developments. In representing nothing less than the material success of an early American dream, food in America became a conspicuous manifestation of independence and the political virtues that informed it. Americans defended access to their food sources and the right to trade their food with the utmost passion during the Revolutionary era. When the British persisted in violating the colonists' most basic constitutional and material rights, the Americans reinvigorated their defense of a hard-earned material way of life by, among many other acts, rioting when merchants tried to sell food at unreasonable prices. The American victory in the Revolutionary War inspired a cultural backlash against the mother country—a conscious rejection of the British culture that Americans had been actively emulating only a decade or so earlier. That rejection led Americans to tout the virtues of the farming life as an explicit cultural and political cause. Thus the virtues of the frontier happily became an animating force in American culture. Food both coincided with and inspired this cultural transition. As Americans idealized a pastoral ideal that stressed such attributes as honestly, frugality, simplicity, lack of pretension, they highlighted the single aspect of geographical and cultural life that Europe lacked: land, land, and more land to replicate the successful creation of a materially rich society. The costs of its development were legendary in terms of the human suffering it caused. Nevertheless, the ownership of a frontier patch of land was the single most important factor in making American food what it was. It was, in essence, what allowed Thomas Jefferson to say with the utmost pride about his new and precarious nation: "how unripe we yet are."

Notes

1 The best overview (also containing a thorough bibliography) of colonial American economic development remains McCusker, J and Menard, R. 1991. *The Economy of British America, 1607–1789*. Chapel Hill, NC: University of North Carolina Press.

2 McCusker and Menard: 58.

3 Klingaman, D. 1971. Food Surpluses and Deficits in the American Colonies, 1768–1772. *The Journal of Economic History*, 31(3): 554.

4 Klingaman: 559.

5 Excellent summaries of the acts and measures passed by the Crown between 1763 and 1773 can be found in Bailyn, B. 1968. *The Ideological Origins of the American Revolution*. Cambridge, MA: Harvard University Press. Also Maier, P., *From Resistance to Revolution: Colonial Radicals and the Development of American Opposition to Britain, 1765–1776* (New York: Norton, 1991).

6 Breen, T. H. 1992. "The Meaning of Things: Interpreting the Consumer Economy in the Eighteenth Century. Brewer, J. and Porter, R. eds. *Consumption and the World of Goods*. New York: Routledge: 250.

7 Smith, B. C. 1994. Food Rioters and the American Revolution. *The William and Mary Quarterly* 51(1): 6.

8 Smith: 6–7.

9 Smith: 8.

10 John Hector St. John Crevecoeur, *Letters from an American Farmer*, Ludvig Lewisohn, ed. (New York: Albert & Charles Boni, 1925): 27.

11 Anderson, F. 1984. *A People's Army: Massachusetts Soldiers and Society in the Seven Years' War*. Chapel Hill, NC: University of North Carolina Press: 87.

12 Brumwell, S. 2002. *Redcoats: The British Soldier and War in the Americas, 1755–1763*. Cambridge: Cambridge University Press: 151–152.

13 Ward, H. M. 1971."*Unite or Die*": *Intercolony Relations, 1690–1763*. Port Washington, NY: Kennikat Press: 77–78.

14 Brumwell: 151–152.

15 Ward: 77.

16 The war's effect on provincial-metropolitan relations is elaborated in Greene, J. P. 1995. *Understanding the American Revolution: Issues and Actors*. Charlottesville, VA: University of Virginia Press: 48–72.

17 Webster, N. 1790. *A Collection of Essays and Fugitive Writings*. Boston, MA: I. Thomas & E. T. Andrews: 3.

18 Quoted in Ellis, J. 1979. *After the Revolution: Profiles of Early American Culture*. New York: Norton: 206.

19 Leonard Labaree (ed.). 1959. *The Papers of Benjamin Franklin*. New Haven, CT: Yale University Press: 16, 140.

20 Crevecoeur: 48–49.

21 Jefferson: 164–165.

22 Crevecoeur: 25.

23 Price, R. 1785. *Observations on the Importance of the American Revolution*. London: T. Cassell: 57–58.

24 Dunlap, W. 1789. *The Father, or American Shantyism*. New York: Hodge, Allen, & Cambell: 3–4.

25 Amelia Simmons.

26 Glasse, H. 1805. *The Art of Cookery Made Plain and Easy.* Alexandria, VA: Cottom & Stewart: 137. The following recipes are from pp. 137–144.

27 Glasse: 112.

28 Glasse: 116.

29 Glasse: 138 and 143.

30 The anecdote comes from Root, W. and De Rochemont, R. 1976. *Eating in America: A History.* New York: Ecco Press: 118.

31 Chasseboeuf, C. F. de, Count of Volney. 1804. *View of the Soil and Climate of the United States of America.* London: J. Johnson: 55.

32 Martineau, H. 1837. *Society in America.* London: Saunders & Otley.

33 Marryat, F. 1839. *A Diary in America.* London: Longmans: 16.

34 Child, L. M. 1838. *The American Frugal Housewife.* New York: Thomas S. & William Wood: 3.

Ashby **Walker**

Emory University

··In the Absence of Food

A CASE OF RHYTHMIC LOSS AND SPOILED IDENTITY FOR PATIENTS WITH PERCUTANEOUS ENDOSCOPIC GASTROSTOMY FEEDING TUBES

This study addresses the social and symbolic meaning of food and explores what happens on a micro/interactional level when people lose the ability to eat. Data are from open-ended survey research questions of patients with percutaneous endoscopic gastrostomy (PEG) feeding tubes as well as their families. Specifically, I draw on the symbolic interactionist perspective to understand the micro/interactional implications of food meaning and how such meanings are intrinsically connected to issues of identity. While eating and receiving proper nourishment are biological necessities for survival, the meanings surrounding eating and various food consumption practices extend far beyond mere nutritional consumption. Partaking in food consumption practices and rituals connects individuals to the societies in which they live. For PEG tube recipients, the loss of the ability to eat is experienced as a social loss and as an event that results in an undesirable change in their identity. Family members of patients with PEG tubes are also affected by this shift in their loved one's identity—indicating a spillover effect of stressful life events from one family member to another. The seemingly banal event of eating is discussed as an extraordinary social phenomenon.

Introduction

Food is a basic part of everyday life. So basic, in fact, that it is easy to overlook its significance as a cultural object. Eating and receiving proper nourishment are biological necessities for survival. The meanings surrounding eating and various food consumption practices, however, extend far beyond mere nutritional consumption. Partaking in food consumption practices and rituals connects individuals to the societies in which they live. Eating is often a social event—it is something that is done with and around other people (Levi-Strauss 1968, 1973; Douglas 1975; Mennell, Murcott and Van Otterloo 1992). Thus, food meaning is connected to interactions with others. In addressing the connection between interaction and food consumption practices, it is impossible to overlook the social elements of identity that are maintained and produced through the cultural events surrounding eating.

In this paper I address the social and symbolic meaning of food and explore what happens when people lose the ability to eat. My research question is "what are the social consequences of losing the ability to eat and how is identity at the micro-level affected by this loss?" To address this research question, I use qualitative survey data collected from a study of patients with percutaneous endoscopic gastrostomy (PEG) feeding tubes. Feeding-tube recipients who have completely lost the ability to eat provide a unique perspective on the meaning of food and identity. Specifically, I draw on the symbolic interactionist perspective to interpret the experiences of the feeding-tube recipients.

Symbolic interactionism is a micro-level theory central to sociological approaches to identity and the presentation of self in everyday life. This paradigm illuminates the ways in which humans use symbols to convey and share meaning in everyday life and places a significant emphasis on the notion of the self (Mead 1934; Charon 1998). Symbolic interactionism posits that the way we feel about and experience ourselves is directly related to the meanings we derive from our interactions with others. Gecas and Burke's (1995: 42) definition of identity comes from a symbolic interactionist perspective:

> Identity refers to who or what one is, to the various meanings attached to oneself by self and others. In sociology, the concept refers both to self-characterizations individuals make in terms of the structural features of group membership, and categories and to the various character traits an individual displays and others attribute to an actor on the basis of his/her conduct ... in a sense, identity is the most public aspect of self.

The use of Gecas and Burke's (1995) definition, in conjunction with the symbolic interactionist conceptualization of the self (Goffman 1959; 1963; Stryker 1980) will serve to frame the analysis presented in this paper.

By drawing on existing works on the social meaning of food, this paper expands previous research on identity nested within the symbolic interactionist tradition by viewing eating as a ritual that is central to self-presentation. Douglas (1975) and Levi-Strauss (1968, 1973) posit that food consumption practices of a given culture provide a ritual link between individuals and larger cultural norms and beliefs. The symbolic meanings surrounding eating as a cultural event also illustrate the ways in which individuals are differentially positioned around food rituals based on status characteristics like gender (Counihan and Kaplan 1998; DeVault 1991; McIntosh and Zey 1998), class (Bourdieu 1984), and race (Witt 1999). Such connections between food and cultural identity have been demonstrated, but research within symbolic interactionism has neglected considering the ritual of eating as a core part of the social self or the centrality of food rituals to relationships among significant others. Throughout this paper I use examples from my data to illustrate the relationship between food and identity and demonstrate how eating as a cultural ritual and process mediates this relationship.

BACKGROUND ON PEG FEEDING TUBES

A PEG is a specific type of feeding tube; PEG stands for percutaneous (through the skin) endoscopic gastrostomy (stomach tube). When patients are unable to nourish themselves orally (due to stroke, head and neck injury, cancer, digestive disease, muscular degenerative disorders etc.), a PEG may be placed through the skin and directly into the stomach. The use of PEG tubes as an alternative to other forms of artificial hydration and nutrition was introduced in 1980 and since that time it has become the most widely used form of enteral feeding (Nicholson *et al.* 2000: 21). The use of PEG tubes was originally intended for short-term intervention in children and neonatal infants facing correctable digestive disorders or disease, but the vast majority of PEG tubes today are used as long-term intervention for elderly individuals with chronic and terminal illnesses (Grant 1998; Nicholson *et al.* 2000; Brett and Rosenberg 2001). By 1990, roughly one out of every 100 hospitalized patients eighty-five years of age or older had a PEG feeding tube (Brett and Rosenberg 2001).

The widespread use of feeding tubes for elderly and often terminally ill and cognitively impaired individuals has led to debate within the medical literature and community (Grant 1998; Verhoef and Rosendaal 2001). A recent article in the *Journal of the American Medical Association* presented the results of a study that investigated the rampant use of PEG tubes for patients with dementia (Finucane, Christmas and Travis 1999). Reasons commonly cited for placing PEG tubes include decreasing the risk of aspiration pneumonia, prolonging survival, and reducing the risk for pressure sores, but the authors reported the following from their study:

> We found no data to suggest that tube feeding improves any of these clinically important outcomes and some data to suggest that it does not. Further, risks are substantial. The widespread practice of tube feeding should be carefully reconsidered, and we believe that for severely demented patients the practice should be discouraged on clinical grounds. (Finucane et al. 1999)

While the advantages of PEG tubes for specific populations (like short-term placement for children or individuals suffering from traumatic injuries that will heal) have been well documented (Nicholson *et al.* 2000), the people who have clinically proven to benefit least from the use of PEG tubes are the ones most likely to get them. Ethical issues have been raised concerning the high number of individuals with cognitive impairment with PEG tubes and the use of "informed consent" in placing them—particularly in nursing homes where PEG placements are common (Meier *et al.* 2001). For patients in nursing homes who have dementia, mealtime can be especially challenging for the often understaffed facilities. Currently the state and federal regulations only require a ratio of one health care professional to twelve patients in long-term care facilities (Bonn 1998). At mealtime, this usually means that one CNA (certified nursing assistant) is responsible for at least twelve patients. Nursing home residents with advanced dementia often require continual prompting to remember to eat and the patients need help with their food. It is not hard to imagine how much easier it would be on the staff if patients that required high levels of care during mealtime had feeding tubes.

In addition to dementia, nursing home placement, and advanced age, risk of receiving a feeding tube has also been correlated with race. African Americans are nine times more likely to receive PEG tubes than whites or any other racial group (Meier et al. 2001). While the ethical implications for the high use of PEG tubes in elderly patients suffering from dementia is broadly contested within the medical literature (noted above), similar discussions about the high use of PEG tubes for African Americans is missing. Here, a sociological analysis is needed to connect the overuse of PEG tubes for blacks with the larger historical and structural discrimination within American health care that has consistently provided differential medical care and treatment for patients according to race (Aldridge & Rodgers-Rose 1993; Williams & Collins 1996; Freund and McGuire 1999).

Also lacking in the medical literature are discussions of the social consequences that reduce the quality of life for patients who lose the ability to eat. Existing research on feeding tubes tends to focus on food as a biological necessity that provides nourishment for the physical body (Murray 1993; Slomka 1995; Bonn 1998; Finucane, Christmas and Travis 1999). Consequently, medical research on PEG tubes focuses on whether or not the tubes extend human life and work biologically rather than dealing with the social implications of feeding tubes. While patients with feeding tubes are still receiving the nutritional material needed to live, they are unable to consume food orally, which is a major social and symbolic event. By focusing on the social meanings of food and the loss of the ability to participate in food consumption practices, this paper will specifically address such oversights in the medical literature and provide evidence that the placement of PEG tubes has undesirable consequences that extend beyond medical/physical considerations.

Methodology

To explore the social consequences of losing the ability to eat, I rely on a study of patients with PEG feeding tubes from a community hospital in a mid-sized southern town. The purpose of the larger hospital study was to examine the expectations of patients and family members about the feeding tubes and to follow the patients' status over a period of six months. The Sheps Research Center at the University of North Carolina at Chapel Hill designed the study and collected data from two locations in the state. As the survey researcher at one of the two locations, I was given permission to use the data that I collected for my own research.

A complete description of the methodology and characteristics of the population is provided in Appendix A, but a brief overview of the research design will be mentioned here to frame the results that follow. The hospital research used a survey containing both open and closed questions concerning patients' experience of PEG tubes. For the purposes of this paper, the answers to open ended questions about the feeding tube were transcribed and analyzed using the qualitative computer program Ethnograph. Through the use of Ethnograph, I was able to sort through open-ended responses of patients and their families and explore the actual content of their experiences with the PEG tubes. Of particular interest to me was how being unable to eat had affected everyday interactions. After entering the data into Ethnograph, I read and reread the responses and developed coding schemes according to themes (integration versus isolation, positive, negative, or neutral descriptions of the tube, etc.). I then compared and interpreted relevant categories in an attempt to locate confirmations as well as contradictions of patterns (Lofland and Lofland 1995).

Eligibility for the PEG study included requirements for patients to be older than twenty-one, for the primary diagnosis not to be head or neck injury, and for the patient or family member responsible for the patient to agree to participate, along with the physician who ordered the PEG tube. Overall, fifty-one patients and family members completed surveys—with the mean age of patients being seventy-three and a median age of seventy-eight. From the sample of fifty-one, I chose a subsample of patients who had completely lost the ability to eat[1] and who were not in a comatose state. Sixteen patients met these criteria and their responses, along with the responses of their family members provided the data for this project. To protect the confidentiality and anonymity of the respondents, their names have been changed when discussed in this paper.

Identity and Food Meaning

Overall, the open-ended responses indicate that the experience with the feeding tube was negative. Words used to describe experiences with the feeding tube included sad, frustrated, depressed, lonely, difficult, hard, angry, mad, deceived, hell, upsetting, and uncomfortable. In nine out of sixteen surveys, patients reported "hating" the tube either through their own responses or the responses of family members for them. When asked "What is the best thing about the tube?" ten answered that it was the only way to keep the patients alive, four said there was nothing good about the tube, and two said they did not know.

SOCIAL LOSS AND IDENTITY CONSEQUENCES

One of the major trends in the feedback provided by patients and family members was that being unable to eat was socially uncomfortable and, as a result, the loss of the ability to eat was experienced as a social bereavement. The loss of the ability to eat not only affects individuals who are unable to eat but it also affects their family and surrogates. In answering the opened-ended questions about the loss of the ability to eat, over half of the respondents said that it made either the surrogate or patient uncomfortable around others. For patients living at home, it was very common for the surrogates to express feelings of guilt about eating and cooking around the patient who was unable to eat. Connie, the wife of Bill (a white male of sixty-two) said: "Around the house it was hard, I didn't want to eat or cook around him and he didn't want friends of family around here visiting because it was uncomfortable for him." Beth, the wife of an eighty-year-old white male called John reported that "I felt bad eating around him—we all felt so bad about it." The patients echoed this sentiment, claiming that they were very aware of how uncomfortable everyone was eating around them. For patients living in nursing homes, there was also a common experience of isolation as a result of the feeding tube as well as diminished social interactions as they were no longer able to attend meals in the facilities' dining halls—one of the few social interactions they usually engaged in.

For individuals who lose the ability to eat, the experience is socially detrimental. As Gecas and Burke (1995: 42) point out, identity is "the most public aspect of self". Individuals eat across all of their identities, regardless of which are more or less salient. As a mother, friend, peer, child, sister, and neighbor—we eat and interact around the shared meanings and rituals that surround food (Lupton 1996). The tendency for individuals to express the loss of the ability to eat as a social loss gives testimony to the public aspect of identity that somehow changes when individuals are unable to eat. The words of Betty, a 67-year-old white female, clearly describe issues in her identity that she experienced as result of the feeding tube placement:

> When I got the tube I was so upset. My whole life I had cooked for my family—I'm good at it and that's what I love to do. I knew the kids wouldn't let me cook for them anymore because they would feel bad—me cooking and not be able to eat nothing. I was upset about not eating food, but not being able to cook anymore made me more upset. It made me feel sad and lonely.

The loss of the ability to eat is particularly difficult for Betty because of her identity as the cook for her family. In her words, "I'm good at it and that's what I love to do." Losing the ability to eat takes away Betty's ability to cook for her family and thus changes the way she and her family define her identity. DeVault (1991) argues that because cooking has traditionally been constructed as female sex-typed task, food preparation in the home has become associated with larger meanings of caring and nurturing behavior and responsibility. Thus, constructions of being a "good" wife and mother become paired with expectations of cooking for the family and loving family members through food-related duties and traditions.

Another example comes from the daughter of Joe, an 82-year-old black male. Joe's daughter Ann expressed sadness over the loss of her father's ability to eat because of the fact that Joe could no longer cook. Ann described the situation as follows:

> You see, he cooked for me and I paid all of the bills and that was like our system. Now that he can't eat he also cannot cook and there was no way I would cook around him or let people bring food into this house. I ate cold cereal three times a day every day from the day he got home from the hospital.

Joe expressed similar concern about being unable to cook for his daughter: "I've got nothing to offer her now. Nothing I can do to give back to her."

Losing the ability to eat had a tremendous impact on Joe's identity. In this example with Joe and his daughter, their "system" was disrupted, as he was no longer able to cook and Joe expressed his sadness over the loss of his part in that system. What also is clear in this example is that individuals who lose the ability to eat and their families often adopt strategies to minimize the impact of the tube placement on their lives. Ann explained that she ate cold cereal so her father could not smell what she was eating. There are several other examples where family members living in the home avoided eating or cooking anything around the person with the feeding tube. Joyce, the wife of one feeding tube recipient lost "over 40 pounds" in the six months following her husband's PEG placement because she felt so badly about eating around him. Also, it was common for social visits involving food to be avoided in order to reduce any social embarrassment.

The common experience of social embarrassment and social discomfort repeatedly talked about by the patients and their families suggests a tension surrounding role-conflicts in situations involving food. An example of this type of tension over social embarrassment is seen in the case of Bill, a 62-year-old white male, who received his feeding tube a month before his only daughter's wedding. In talking about the tube, Bill and his wife considered in great detail if he could handle sitting at the head table and not eating or not being able to try a piece of his daughter's wedding cake. Bill also expressed concern about how "ridiculous" it would look to have the tube bulging out from underneath his tuxedo. Bill faced a conflict in his identity as father of the bride and wedding party member with his role of the individual who was unable to eat. Bill ultimately decided not to attend the wedding reception or rehearsal dinner. Withdrawing from the social situations that involved food and eating was a very common coping mechanism for the patients and their families in this study. Stryker (1980) lists withdrawal as one way of dealing with role conflict, as individuals seek to reduce stress created from an inability to align different aspects of their social selves. Because losing the ability to eat has a tremendous impact on individuals' identities, it is no surprise that the loss of the ability to eat results in social loss and retraction from social situations.

A particularly interesting example of identity issues for participants in the PEG study is found in the story of Jack, an 86-year-old white male. Jack returned home to live with his wife after receiving his feeding tube. In contrast to the previous examples of patients who mourned the loss of the ability to cook for others, Jack was bothered by the fact that no one was cooking *for* him. He chose to handle the situation in a unique way:

> [Jack] I still sit at the table at mealtime with food in front of me—we have mealtime just the same time like we used to—only now I can't eat. But I've tried to keep things as they always were.
>
> [Jack's Wife] He still makes me cook for him, even knowing he can't eat it. I think he still feels like the man around here when he can tell me what to cook. We sit at the table and he makes me put his plate in front of him—but I feel so uncomfortable eating around him.

Here, Jack's wife's words, "he still feels like the man" describe the maintenance of gender identity within the household. By having his wife cook for him and by sitting at the table during mealtime, Jack said he tried to "keep things as they always were." This provides an extremely pertinent example of the ways in which the loss of the ability to eat affect individual identity and of the ways in which individuals seek to keep consistency within those identities despite the inconsistencies that develop with the loss of the ability to eat.

TEMPORAL RHYTHMS OF EATING AND IDENTITY

Jack's description of his desire to "keep things as they always were" raises a second important theme in the discussion of food and identity: the patterns and rhythms that surround food consumption practices. Zerubavel's (1981) work on the sociology of time and sociotemporal rhythms provides useful insight into understanding how eating can serve as social rhythm and temporal structure for individuals. Zerubavel (1981: 2) divides the dimensions of temporal profiles of situations into four categories: the sequential structure (the steps and order in which events occur), duration, temporal location (a set time something occurs), and rate of recurrence (how often something should occur or its rhymicity). We have a deeply embedded awareness of how, when, where, and what should happen in our daily lives and eating is one those events. While eating might be tied to biological necessity it is more often shaped by our rigid structuring of mealtime and eating activities. "Thus, we eat usually not necessarily when we are hungry but rather during officially designated eating periods such as 'lunchtime' or 'dinnertime'" (Zerubavel 1981: 7). These designated times and patterns not only help us divide our days but also connect us to the social structure in which we live.

How is eating as a pattern and social rhythm tied to our identity? The answer can be found in Stryker's (1980) definition of social structure and identity rooted within the symbolic interactionist tradition. Stryker (1980: 65) defines identity as something that is deeply connected to social structure:

> To involve the idea of social structure is to refer to the patterned regularities that characterize most human interaction. Whatever may be true of the creative potential or persons in their interactions with one another, as matter of empirical fact most of their interactions tend to be with the same or only slowly changing cast of others, and the same sets of persons tend to be bound together or linked in interactional networks doing essentially the same things on, a repetitive basis.

For patients who lose the ability to eat, they lose the ability to be connected to particular social positions through the patterned regularity of eating. Specifically, they lose this patterned regularity with the most intimate set of people in their lives.

One of the ways time is organized for individuals is through the rituals and rhythms of holidays and special celebrations. In keeping with Douglas' (1975) assertion that food consumption practices are ordered as courses within meals, meals within weeks, and festivities within years, some of the participants in the sample mentioned and reflected on specific holidays and special meal events in relation to their inability to eat. For Ben, a 63-year-old white male, getting his tube out in time for Thanksgiving was a priority because, in his words, "what is Thanksgiving without Turkey and stuffing yourself silly/full?" Other patients and families mentioned birthdays, Christmas, and special weekly meals as events that had been somehow changed due to the inability to eat. For these individuals, the loss of the ability to eat was felt particularly intensely around special events that centered on food. For other individuals, the loss of the ability to eat severed them from the only meaningful routine they had left.

For individuals living in long-term care facilities like nursing homes, mealtime is one of the few events that mimics life as they knew it outside of the institution (Zerubavel 1981; Arber and Evandrou 1993). In such an institutional setting, mealtime is one of the only meaningful structures that provides individuals with any kind of temporal and social regularity. In two instances, surrogates spoke about losing the ability to eat in relation to time and routines. One wife commented: "He wants to eat! He loves to eat! What else does an old man in a nursing home have to do with all that time?" The daughter of another PEG recipient commented: "In the nursing home mealtime [is] very important. It [is] their social function. My mother had her friends she sat by everyday and it was such an important routine for her ... she lost out on all of that ... the mealtime organized their days." For patients in nursing homes, the "patterned regularity" of eating links them to their identities in the larger social structure.

Patients living at home faced similar issues and their loss of the ability to eat was frequently discussed in terms of time. Jason, a 28-year-old white male commented: "All I do is lay here all day watching TV with all those food commercials. What else do I have to do other than eat?"

Betty, a 67-year-old white female, remarked: "It's much harder to know what time it is anymore. I mean, I used to just know based on when I would eat or when it was time to start preparing the meals for the kids 'cuz they used to come eat over here all the time. Now the days just seem like one big thing."

Because PEG tube recipients are dealing with a number of other health problems and complications, there are few events that structure their days in a meaningful way outside of their illness. While Jason mentioned watching television, he talked about it in terms of the food commercials that just reminded him of what he was *unable* to do. Because Jason was bedridden due to his severe muscular dystrophy, he went on to explain that eating food was one of the few things he looked forward to throughout the day. And for Betty, the loss of the ability to eat as well as to cook disrupted her sense of time altogether.

For most PEG patients who lost the ability to eat there were no real options for changing the eating situation. Many withdrew from social settings involving food or modified existing behavior to minimize the effect of being unable to eat but none of these solutions changed the meaning of food for identity in the larger social structure. Instead of changing their situation, individuals were faced with a new identity—a stigmatized or spoiled identity.

SPOILED IDENTITY
::

Goffman (1963) explores the issues of stigmatized identity and how these identities emerge when persons are unable to conform to standards that society considers "normal." One type of stigmatized identity is that of "abominations of the body" (Goffman 1963: 4) where individuals have some type of physical deformity. The feeding tube is a visible and alien fixture to the human body and can be seen as a physical deformity that results in a stigma in and of itself. Goffman (1963: 43–44) describes such stigma symbols as "signs which are especially effective in drawing attention to a debasing identity discrepancy, breaking up what would otherwise be a coherent overall picture, with a consequent reduction in our valuation of the individual." It was very common for individuals to list the tube itself as a problem with losing the ability to eat because of its intrusive design. The comment of John's (an eighty-year-old white male) about the nuisance of the tube are representative of the frustrations that were commonly associated with the tube for patients in the study: "The way the tube is designed is one of the worst things about it. It always gets in my way. My wife and I have learned how to tie it tight against me with a long shoestring. But even then, you see it under my shirt."

There was no way to hide the tube effectively under their clothes or to conceal the process that surrounds tube feedings. Also, the physical side effects from the tube were troublesome as well. The daughter of Helen (a 78-year-old black female) explained her concerns about the port where the tube entered her mother's stomach:

> It smells awful where the tube goes in her stomach ... it's all crusty and gross. There is something wrong with the way they put that tube in, because it always leaks everywhere on her clothes. That's why those nurse assistants won't go in her room. It's gross and they don't want to deal with the mess they put her in.

Helen's daughter attributed the lack of care her mother was getting with the negative and socially undesirable consequences of the PEG tube. The placement of the PEG tube added a stigmatized symbol to the patients' identity that was not present in their lives before. But not being able to eat was a stigma above and beyond the presence of the tube.

In considering the dimensions of stigma surrounding the loss of the ability to eat and the presence of the PEG tube in patients' lives, another interesting trend in the data was for patients to mourn the loss of eating what they referred to as "real" food. This response by Bill is representative of these types of answers: "I wanted to eat—I mean chew and swallow real food. I knew with my mind that I was getting some nutrition through my tube but have you seen that stuff? It's just liquid mush, not real food."

Other similar answers included: "He wants steak and real food. Puree food isn't real to him." "It was really hard not to be able to eat real food." "He wanted real food. He wanted to eat so bad." "She wants her real food like Good-N-Plenty and Fritos corn chips."

Other foods patients missed included fast food, greens, ice-cream, barbecue, chicken and fish. Technically, the patients were receiving nourishment through their tubes. However, the family and patients did not conceptualize the liquid nourishment that bypassed the mouth and went directly into the stomach as eating. By repeatedly differentiating between real food and the feeding tube, the patients defined the liquid nourishment as something other than real and void of authentic food status. The tube and liquid nourishment were not able to substitute for the cultural event of eating, or for the meanings associated with foods as specific symbols. Overall, the liquid nourishment delivered via the intrusion of the plastic tube was a process that violated social meanings and boundaries of selfhood connected to eating (Levi-Strauss 1970; Lupton 1996; Douglas 2002)

By not being able to eat, the individuals who received the feeding tubes were unable to conform to the world around them. The fact that many individuals made attempts to minimize this loss can be described as efforts at "covering" the stigmatized identity. Goffman (1963: 102) depicts "covering" as follows: "The individual's objective is to reduce tension, that is to make it easier for himself and for the others to withdraw covert attention from the stigma and to sustain spontaneous involvement in the official content of the interaction." There were multiple examples of this type of behavior where both the tube recipients and their families tried to hide or camouflage the fact that they were unable to eat. Several examples were mentioned earlier about surrogates not wanting to eat in front of their loved ones who had the PEG tubes but there were also examples of patients who tried to avoid making their loved ones uncomfortable as well. Ben, who lived on the same street as his extended family clearly describes his efforts at covering:

> I'm real close with my son and his wife and they live on my street and she always cooks and I go down there every week, but when I had the tube I didn't even go near the house around meal time because I didn't want them feeling bad. I would always have a real good excuse, but they probably knew what I was doing. But even if they did, I think it made us all feel better.

Conclusion

The results and trends from this limited sample cannot be generalized to the entire population of patients who receive PEG feeding tubes or to people who lose the ability to eat under different circumstances. However, these data do provide insight concerning how the inability to eat affects people. Returning to the theoretical concepts presented earlier in the text and the framework of symbolic interactionism it is clear that the loss of the ability to eat has a significant effect on social interactions and identity. It is not just the case that losing the ability to eat changes the individuals' identities, but it gives them a *stigmatized* identity and this identity shift has severe consequences for the individuals and their families.

The fact that a PEG tube is considered a "feeding tube" is significant when considering how the medical community conceptualizes food and eating. Slomka (1995) asserts that artificial nutrition and hydration cannot be considered as food but rather must be seen as a medical treatment. Slomka's (1995) discussion forces a reconsideration of the meaning that the label "feeding tube" invokes and the conflict between the way the tube is named and the actual experience of the feeding tube. The results presented in this paper provide strong support for Slomka's claims.

When considering the undesirable consequences of PEG tubes, it is vital to point out that these tubes are being imposed upon blacks at higher rates than whites. The placement of a feeding tube results in an inability to eat—an inability to participate in a highly salient cultural ritual. Here, not being able to eat serves as a symbolic boundary of exclusion (Levi-Strauss 1970; Douglas 1975, 2002). Because this exclusion process is occurring at higher rates for blacks, it is necessary to examine the underlying reasons for this phenomenon within the medical community. Current medical research identifies and acknowledges that blacks receive PEG tubes at higher rates than any other racial group (Meier *et al.* 2001)—this research, however, fails to address the implications of this reality. Future research on PEG tubes needs to include a more thoughtful consideration of their overuse within the black community and confront the larger issues of unequal healthcare that continue to plague our medical system.

While the medical community needs to address the social implications of PEG tubes, the social psychology literature rooted in symbolic interactionism can be enriched by further investigation of food as a social and symbolic resource and by addressing how important seemingly banal events like eating are in maintaining a "normal" and non-stigmatized identity. While completely losing the ability to eat is an extreme circumstance, there are many less drastic examples of interruptions in 'typical' eating behavior that warrant attention and further thought. Individuals with diabetes or other medical conditions who are forced to modify or change their diets may face similar identity-related issues when they find themselves unable to participate fully in certain food consumption practices that are highly visible culturally. If food is defined as a social and symbolic resource, conditions like obesity or anorexia can be explored from a perspective where an over or under consumption of food represents a specific identity struggle with a very potent cultural object. Or, an inequality in the distribution of food as a cultural resource among individuals can result in a differentiation of status characteristics—for young children in elementary school, an awareness of who is on a "free-lunch" program might result in the stigmatization of certain children that could have devastating consequences for identity formation and maintenance.

Overall, addressing the social consequences of the loss of the ability to eat is useful because it illuminates the importance of being able to eat "normally" which is commonly overlooked in discussions of identity. Stryker (1980) refers to common events that punctuate everyday life as "patterned regularities" but they can also be thought of as rituals. The study of eating as a ritual can provide a bridge between several interrelated disciplines within sociology and may even represent fertile ground for the exploration of micro-macro connections between individuals and their social structures. Further research that actually attempts to identify and empirically examine the social significance of food consumption practices could provide a rich discussion that would merge the cultural literature with the social psychological literature in a much-needed way. Such regularities and rituals are perhaps so commonplace in daily living that it is difficult to identify them as important social events or elements of identity structure. In the case of food, it becomes painfully clear how vital it is socially only when one loses the ability to eat. At times, it is not until the absence of something is recognized that the implications of its presence can be fully understood.

Acknowledgments

Data come from a study of PEG patients by the Sheps Research Center at Chapel Hill. (principal investigator on the project, Nancy Phifer, MD, to whom I am indebted.) A special thanks to Julie Brown of the University of North Carolina at Greensboro for guiding me through this thesis project. I thank Cathryn Johnson, Karen Hegtvedt, and Nikki Khanna of Emory University for their their feedback on recent drafts of the paper—along with the helpful reviews of contributors from *FCS*.

Appendix A: Methodology

The hospital research on which these data were based used a survey containing both open and closed questions and took about thirty minutes to complete. The survey contained forty-seven closed questions and seven open questions that asked patients/families about their expectations of the feeding tubes, their actual experience with the feeding tubes, their physical and mental well-being, and basic demographic information. The survey was either done in person or over the telephone depending on what was most convenient for the patients and their families. Three surveys were conducted with each patient. The first survey was carried out at the time of the PEG placement, the second survey was conducted at three months following the PEG placement, and the third survey was performed at six months following the PEG placement. The same basic questions were asked in all three surveys. Patients and family members were informed of the purpose of the study and were also told that participation was voluntary and their decision regarding participation would in no way alter their medical care or treatment.

The population for this study was recruited from the hospital, and patients were eligible for the study under the following conditions: (1) the doctor who ordered the PEG placement agreed to let the patient be surveyed; (2) the patient was a first-time PEG recipient; (3) the primary diagnosis of the patient was not head or neck injury; (4) the patient was twenty-one or older; (5) the patient or family member agreed to participate. The survey was conducted with the patient who received the PEG if he or she was mentally capable. If the patient was not able to participate, the person closest to the patient was surveyed instead. Participation in the study by a surrogate was only allowed if the person claiming to be a surrogate was actively involved in the patient's daily life and care.

Because I was investigating the interactions surrounding food consumption practices and how the identity of the tube recipient was affected it was important to know how the people closest to the recipient experienced that identity shift as well. Based on the definition of identity provided by Gecas and Burke (1995: 42), which emphasizes "the various meanings attached to oneself by self and others", and the symbolic interactionist notion of meaning being inherently linked to interaction with others, surveys from the patient or the surrogate were equally valuable. Both patient and family are involved in the rituals and meanings surrounding food.

Fifty-one patients completed baseline surveys and the overall response rate for enrollment in the study for eligible participants was 89%. A demographic snapshot of the fifty-one patients in the PEG study shows that this population was predominantly elderly, with slightly more men than women and with an overrepresentation of African Americans. The range of ages for patients in the PEG study was twenty-eight to ninety-three, with a mean age of seventy-three and a median age of seventy-eight, with twenty-eight being a definite outlier. Of the fifty-one patients, twenty-nine (57%) were men and twenty-two (43%) were women. Despite the fact that there were five different categories for self-reported race along with an open-ended blank for "other", the only two reported races were white and African-American with thirty-four (67%) white participants and seventeen (33%) African-American participants.[2]

The vast majority of the surveys were conducted with surrogates (forty surrogate surveys) and the minority with patients (eleven patient surveys). Thirty-three out of the forty surrogate surveys were conducted with female surrogates and only seven with male surrogates. The types of surrogate relationships in order of their frequency were a daughter caring for a parent (seventeen), a wife caring for a husband (twelve), a son caring for a parent (four), a husband caring for a wife (two), a niece caring for an aunt (two), a brother caring for a brother (one), a mother caring for a son (one), and a granddaughter caring for a grandfather (one). The three cases that included an extended family member (grandchild or niece) as surrogate were all black respondents.

SELECTION AND CODING OF THE SPECIFIC POPULATION SAMPLE: A SAMPLE WITHIN A SAMPLE

: :

Because this paper deals with the loss of the ability to eat only the surveys from patients who had completely lost the ability to eat were explored. In order to identify patients who had completely lost the ability to eat, answers to the closed question "Do you consider the feeding tube a supplement to eating or a replacement to eating?" were examined. Of the fifty-one patients, twenty-nine participants considered the tube a replacement to eating, twenty-one said that they considered the tube a supplement to eating, and one answered that he did not know. The analysis here focuses on the respondents who indicated that the PEG tube was a total replacement to eating and who were not in a comatose state. Sixteen patients meet these criteria and their responses, along with the responses of their family members provided the data for this research.

The demographics of the sixteen cases included in this research mirrored those of the larger sample and were representative of the trends in gender, race, and age. There were more men than women (ten men and six women), twelve of the respondents were white and four were black, there was a mean age of seventy-one, and a median age of seventy-six. The age range for the population remained at twenty-eight to ninety-three because the oldest and youngest respondents from the larger data set were both in the smaller data set. Like the larger sample, there were more surrogate surveys than patient surveys with nine surrogate surveys, three patient surveys, and four combined patient and surrogate survey (resulting in twenty overall respondents speaking about the experience of sixteen patients). At the time of the baseline survey, nine patients were living at home with a surrogate, four were in nursing homes, and three were in extended care facilities. By the time of the most recent follow-up survey, twelve patients still had the feeding tube, two did not have the feeding tube any more, and two patients had died.

Institutional Review Board constraints with the hospital study meant that I was only able to add two open-ended questions to the survey. They were:

(1) "How has being unable to eat made you/your family member feel?" and (2) "How has being unable to eat affected you/your family member's interactions with others?" These questions were added to the three- and six-month follow up surveys and were presented to the patients and their families as part of the hospital study. The intent of adding these two questions was to address the theoretical issues raised by a symbolic interactionist approach to food. Both of these questions gave patients and family members a chance to reflect on the loss of the ability to eat. In providing patients/family members with the opportunity to talk about micro/interactional issues surrounding eating, I was able to link food meaning to cultural context. These questions also addressed issues of identity with the loss of the ability to eat.

It is important to note that as a healthy, white female in my early twenties who had never experienced life with a feeding tube of any sort, my positionality placed me in several outgroup categories from the people I was surveying. While I do not know the extent to which my characteristics affected the data collection process, I do know that who I am as a researcher affects both the information people give me as well as my interpretation of that information and it is vital to recognize this. I would argue that one of the reasons for the high response rate in the hospital study was the fact that people considered me to be a "legitimate" part of the hospital staff. While I was employed by the hospital, my job was only that of a survey-researcher and even though this was explained it was common for people to ask me very technical medical questions about how to care for the tube or how to get in touch with their primary care physician so they could get the tube out and so on.

I also found people willing to talk about the tube due to their frustrations with the PEG and a desire to voice their complaints. I am extremely grateful for the time people were willing to take to answer the questions in this survey. The majority of the individuals in this study were facing an extreme crisis in their health and often dealing with the reality of their own terminal illness or that of a loved one, and the time that they gave was one of the most precious things they had to offer. The patients and their families provided rich feedback and their input yielded a story with common and overlapping themes that provided the data for this paper.

Notes

1. The paper deals with the loss of the ability to eat so I did not want to include patients who were able to eat some food orally. Some patients in the study had PEG tubes for supplemental eating as opposed to a complete replacement for eating.
2. The racial composition of the PEG respondents was mostly in keeping with the demographics of the larger area from which the surveys were completed—with a slight

overrepresentation of African Americans. The absence of any participants with a self-reported race of "Hispanic, non-white" could be due to a number of factors, including the fact that the mean age of Hispanic non-white individuals in the area was significantly lower than the mean age of the PEG tube recipients in this study, and an overall lack of access to medical care.

References

: :

ALDRIDGE, D. P. and RODGERS-ROSE, L. (eds). 1993. *River of Tears: The Politics of Black Women's Health*. Newark, NJ: Traces Publishing.

ARBER, S. and EVANDROU, M. (eds). 1993. *Ageing, Independence and the Life Course* London: Jessica Kingsley Publishers.

BONN, K. 1998. Feeding Tubes: Whose Decision? *Nursing Homes Long Term Care Management* 47: 80–81.

BOURDIEU, P. 1984. *Distinction: a Social Critique of the Judgment of Taste*. Translated by Richard Nice. Cambridge, MA: Harvard University Press.

BRETT, A. S. and ROSENBERG, J. 2001. The Adequacy of Informed Consent for Placement of Gastrostomy Tubes. *Archives of Internal Medicine* 161: 745–748.

CHARON, J. 1998. *Symbolic Interactionism: An Introduction, An Integration*. Upper Saddle River, NJ: Prentice-Hall.

COUNIHAN, C. and KAPLAN, S. 1998. *Food and Gender: Identity and Power*. Amsterdam: Harwood Academic Publishers.

DEVAULT, M. 1991. *Feeding the Family*. Chicago, IL: Chicago University Press.

DOUGLAS, M. [1975] 1997. Deciphering a Meal. In C. Counihan and S. Kaplan (eds) *Food and Culture: A Reader*. New York: Routledge.

——— 2002. *Purity and Danger: An Analysis of the Concept of Pollution and Taboo*. New York: Routledge.

FINUCANE, T., CHRISTMAS, C. and TRAVIS, K. 1999. Tube Feeding in Patients with Advanced Dementia. *Journal of the American Medical Association* 282: 1365–1370.

FREUND, P. S. and McGUIRE, M. B. 1999. *Health, Illness and the Social Body*. Upper Saddle River, NJ: Prentice-Hall.

GECAS, V. and BURKE, P. 1995. Self and Identity. K. Cook, o-. House and G. Fine (eds) *Sociological Perspectives on Social Psychology*, pp. 41–67. New York: Harcourt College Publishers.

GOFFMAN, E. 1959. *The Presentation of Self in Everyday Life*. New York: Doubleday.

——— 1963a. *Behavior in Public Places: Notes on the Social Organization of Gatherings*. New York: The Free Press.

——— 1963b. *Stigma: Notes on the Management of Spoiled Identity*. New York: Simon & Schuster.

GRANT, M. 1998. Gastrostomies in Older Patients: The 1990 Hospital Discharge Survey. *Journal of the American Board of Family Practice* 11: 187–192.

LEVI-STRAUSS, C. 1968. *The Origin of Table Manners*. Translated by John and Doreen Weightman. New York: Oxford University Press.

——— 1970. *The Raw and the Cooked*. Translated by John and Doreen Weightman. London: Jonathan Cape.

——— 1973. *From Ashes to Honey*. Translated by John and Doreen Weightman. New York: Oxford University Press.

LOFLAND, J. and LOFLAND, L. 1995. *Analyzing Social Settings: A Guide to Qualitative Observations and Analysis*. Belmont, CA: Wadsworth.

LUPTON, D. 1996. *Food, the Body and the Self*. Thousand Oaks, CA: Sage.

McINTOSH, A. and ZEE, M. 1998. Women as Gatekeepers of Food Consumption: A Sociological Critique. C. Counihan and S. Kaplan (eds) *Food and Gender: Identity and Power* Amsterdam: Harwood Academic Publishers.

MEAD, G. H. 1934. *Mind, Self and Society*. Chicago, IL: University of Chicago Press.

MEIER, D. E., AHRONHEIM, J., MORRIS, J., BASKIN-LYONS, S. and MORRIS, R. S. 2001. High Short Term Mortality in Hospitalized Patients with Advanced Dementia: Lack of Benefit of Tube Feeding. *Archives of Internal Medicine* 161: 594–599.

MENNELL, S., MURCOTT, A. and VAN OTTERLOO, A. 1991. *The Sociology of Food: Eating, Diet and Culture*. Newbury Park: Sage.

Murray, M. 1993. Principles of Caring for Residents with Feeding Tubes. *Nursing Homes Long Term Care Management* 42: 37–40.

Nicholson, F. B., Korman, M. G. and Richardson, M. 2000. 'Percutaneous Endoscopic Gastrostomy: A Review of Indication, Complication and Outcome. *Gastroenterology and Hepatology* 15: 21–25.

Slomka, J. 1995. What do Apple Pie and Motherhood have to do with Feeding Tubes and Caring for the Patient?" *Archives of Internal Medicine* 155: 1258–1263.

Stryker, S. 1980. *Symbolic Interactionism*. Menlo Park, CA: Benjamin/Cummings.

Verhoef, M. J. and Van Rosendaal, G. 2001. Patient Outcomes Related to Percutaneous Endoscopic Gastrostomy Placement. *Journal of Clinical Gastroenterology* 32(1): 49–53.

Williams, D. R. and Collins, C. 1996. U.S. Socioeconomic and Racial Differences in Health: Patterns and Explanation. P. Brown (ed.) *Perspectives in Medical Sociology*, 2nd edn, pp. 5–43. Prospect Heights, IL: Waveland Press.

Witt, D. 1999. *Black Hunger: Food and the Politics of US Identity*. New York: Oxford University Press.

Zerubavel, E. 1981. *Hidden Rhythms: Schedules and Calendars in Social Life*. Chicago, IL: University of Chicago Press.

LuAnne K. **Roth**

University of Missouri

·· "Beef. It's What's for Dinner"

Vegetarians, Meat-Eaters and the Negotiation of Familial Relationships

While many scholars have explored the celebratory role of food traditions—how food is used to create *communitas*—few consider how food may also be used to punish, cajole, or reinforce hegemonic or patriarchal structures. Drawing on qualitative interviews with vegetarians, I explore the transformation to vegetarianism and the ensuing conflicts between the "homeostasis" of family meat-eating traditions and the "deviance" of refusing meat that are enacted via the family meal. By examining how the inversely related food ideologies of vegetarianism and meat-eating are expressed in this context, a theory arises as to how food behavior and ideology may function to negotiate power, belonging, and exclusion in familial relationships.

> What is patriotism but the love of the good things we ate in our childhood.
>
> Lin Yutang

A number of folklorists and food scholars have explored food's expressiveness, emphasizing the role of food in fostering *communitas*, nurturance, identity, and aesthetics.[1] For the most part, these studies focus on how foodways function to bond family members together. Several scholars have suggested that food is one of the first tools used to negotiate power relations, particularly between parent and child (for example, Bossard 1943; Babcock 1948; Newton 1992), crucial even to the development of the self's subjectivity (Kristeva 1982). These negotiations are not always positive, however, nor do they necessarily lead to social cohesion. Except to give a passing nod to alternative approaches, in fact, too few studies regarding the social aspects of food move beyond its celebratory functions to consider how food behavior may also be used to reinforce hegemonic or patriarchal structures, to punish or cajole, to resist and subvert, or to otherwise negotiate power relations.[2]

Based on qualitative interviews and ethnographic observation, this article attempts to redress this neglected area of foodways scholarship. Examining the etiological stories of vegetarians, which become a vital part of their storytelling repertoire—stories of how and why they became vegetarian—I explore the emergent nature of the process by which they chose to "violate" family food traditions, and that of the dominant meat-eating culture, by eschewing meat. What strikes me most about these stories is that what frequently begins, seemingly, as a food preference becomes explicitly ideological, later incorporating central concerns about health, ecology, humanitarianism, and spirituality. That is, in many cases the meat that suddenly seemed inexplicably "gross" later comes to mean other things, contributing to the discourse in food studies about how food likes and dislikes develop (Angyal 1941; Douglas 1966, 1975; Palmerino 1981; Farb and Armelagos 1983).

If these personal experience narratives typically begin with an explanation of why the individual became vegetarian, their depiction of familial reactions to their alternative eating behavior illustrates the extent to which food choices create and express identity and worldview between individuals and groups.[3] Changes in food behavior are initially viewed by family members as deviant, strange, or crazy—a threat to the family's "homeostasis," its traditions, and its group identity—and thus, the changes are resisted (often very strongly) by members of the family system. The ensuing conflict, then, forms the basis for the negotiation of relationships, played out repeatedly over the family meal. This drama becomes literary when incorporated into the etiological personal experience narratives that are performed quite often—for example, whenever and wherever someone notices the individual refusing meat.

Why They Became Vegetarians
: :

The vast majority of vegetarians I interviewed, when asked why they became vegetarian, described themselves having "problems" eating meat for no apparent reason other than it suddenly looked, tasted, and/or seemed conceptually "gross" at the time.[4] To some extent, this contradicts existing research that cites health and ethical reasons as the primary motivations for becoming vegetarian (e.g., Jabs *et al.* 1998a and b). Consider Michael's account of the single event that spurred his decision:

> Well, it always goes back to this moment when I was sitting at my parent's kitchen table eating dinner. And huh ... I was eating a chicken leg. And I just kinda looked at it. And picked it up ... and looked at it ... and just thought [laughs], "This is disgusting. I can't believe I'm eating this. Put ... it ... down!" And that was the moment, I think, I decided. (Interview, September 2002)

Similar narratives by the majority of vegetarians with whom I spoke recounted how the individual became suddenly and inexplicably "grossed-out," deciding then and there to stop eating meat, or to eat only select "less gross" kinds of meat (e.g., fish and maybe chicken). In some cases, however, a more gradual buildup of aversions is reported. Possibly the same could be said of most vegetarians, but that, years later, a sort of "alchemy of mind" inheres, in which all related thoughts and experiences during the time of the pivotal decision-making period become conflated into one story, boiling down multiple events into one defining moment (see Zeitlin 1980).

Proposing a theory about how food aversions develop, Claire Palmerino's study shows that, "When consumption is followed by negative visceral feedback (e.g., nausea, gastrointestinal upset), the palatability of the food decreases," constituting "a unique form of associative learning" (Palmerino 1981: 20; see also Beardsworth and Keil 1991). Biting into bone fragments or veins, therefore, and the nausea that results, may lead to aversions. This notion makes good sense but a minor distinction must be noted. In many cases, there is a psychological construction of disgust (Vollmecke 1986), a cognitive association that suddenly produces the negative visceral reaction—the realization that they are eating a dead animal, thoughts about how the animal was killed, or in a few instances, thoughts about what else is in meat (e.g., chemicals, hormones, antibiotics, ecologically unsound grazing practices, cruelty, "bad vibes," and so forth). Howard, for instance, was "accustomed to eating gross food" in his college dining hall. One day he bit into a bratwurst, however, and had an extremely negative visceral reaction. "It was huge and dripping with grease," he explains, "I felt my arteries going 'crunch!' I immediately threw it away and ate cereal instead" (Interview, May 1995).

For a few of those individuals I interviewed, reading materials or hearing about factory farming, nutrition, ecological, and humanitarian considerations prompted their decision.[5] In spite of these few cases where concerns over health, ecology, and morality initiated the decision to become vegetarian, for most it was a negative visceral feedback, a gag reflex, a feeling of nausea, a particularly negative mouth feel that quickly brought up cognitive and later emotional associations connecting the killing of animals with the meat being chewed. Put simply, they were suddenly "grossed out" and, according to their "alchemized" narratives, many decided right then never to eat meat again.

The proverb "we are what we eat" suggests that eating "produces a particularly intimate identification with the consumed product" (cf. Guttierez 1984; Georges 1984; Kalčik 1984; Witt 1998; Heldke 2001). "The eating of meat," Julie Twigg suggests, "involves a literal incorporation of the animal, and as such presents us with the ambivalences and complexities of our own attitudes to animals and the animal, nature and the natural" (Twigg 1983:18). Yet, in the few exceptions to the "gross out" factor, where it was ecological or health issues that first influenced their decision, the end result was very similar—a decided distaste for animal flesh—an actual change in taste/distaste. These vegetarian narratives would seem to suggest that regardless of which came first—the mouth feel or disgusting cognitive associations causing the "gross out"—in the end both become inextricably linked as food aversions, around which a coherent ideology developed. Consider Becky's explanation: "Once I decided out of the 'gross factor' I wasn't gonna eat it again, then I became … then I became moral about it"

(Interview, March 1995). Christina's account parallels this as well when she says, "I was in seventh or eighth grade and my best friend had become a vegetarian (I don't know why she did), but we had decided together that meat was gross [laughs]. And it was kinda, I think, an independence thing." Later, though, Christina became involved in environmental activism in high school, during which she learned about the "misuse of land that could be used more efficiently to grow produce, or what have you." The ethical issues came after the fact of her becoming vegetarian, however, and she makes it clear that those issues alone would not have made her decide, even expressing some guilt that she did not "do it for the right reasons" (Interview, September 2002).[6]

According to Twigg's structural analysis, vegetarianism represents a "cultural unity" in terms of ideology. Although the phenomenon is diverse, she finds its coherence embodied in four traditional foci: health, animal welfare, economy/ecology, and spirituality. As interconnected entities, these foci draw strength and sensibility from one another

> Thus the wrongness of exploiting animals relates also to the wrongness of exploiting the Third World. The ecological arguments concerning the devastation of nature and the destruction of animal species relate both to the rights of animals to exist and to essentially "spiritual" conceptions of the whole and of the balance of Man within Nature. (Twigg 1983: 20)

Although interestingly, Twigg ignores the crucial role taste and aversions play in the development of vegetarian ideology, the experiences of my vegetarian interviewees validate aspects of Twigg's structural analysis. Even when the change in eating habits emerges corporeally as a result of negative visceral experiences, therefore, it begins to evolve into a full-fledged ideology. Once they began avoiding meat due to the "gross-out factor," ethical, moral, ecological, and spiritual considerations soon followed.

Food communicates using a rich symbolic language, if you will, through its color, texture, smell, and taste, and through its combination with other foods. Theorists such as Mary Douglas (1975) and Roland Barthes ([1961] 1997) present food as a system that, like language, has its own grammatical structure. If food is structured like language it is crucial to consider vegetarianism as an alternative discourse within the larger language and discourse of the dominant meat-eating culture and, especially in the case of my interviewees, within the context of the "typical midwestern American meat-and-potatoes" family meal where the clash of ideologies is enacted. Structurally speaking, Western vegetarianism inverts the dominant meat-eating culture. Meat-eating ideology places red meat at the top of a hierarchical pyramid where it is given highest status, around which the meal is arranged, and standing "for the very idea of food itself" (Twigg 1983: 21). Grains/vegetables/fruit are then positioned at the bottom where they are regarded as "weak," "insufficient for the formation of a meal, and merely ancillary" (Twigg 1983: 22). Reversing this structure, vegetarian ideology places grains, nuts, and raw fruits and vegetables at the top—the center around which the meal is formed. In its reversal, vegetarianism both draws on and disrupts traditional attitudes and beliefs about meat, creating a symbolic inversion.

Vegetarianism involves both subtle and not-so-subtle "redefinitions" for the meaning of meat, for example meat's traditional association with masculinity is reversed: "Meat can here stand not for maleness in an approved sense, but for what is seen as false, macho stereotype of masculinity. Thus 'strength' and 'power' becomes 'cruelty' and 'aggression'; masculine vigour and courage become violence and the forces of human destructiveness" (Twigg 1983: 27). It is in this vein that Warren Belasco observes about vegetarianism in the 1960s and 1970s:

> Also, perhaps simplifying one's diet to a few "Oriental" staples (brown rice and soy products) symbolized solidarity with poor but spiritually strong Vietnamese peasants. The soybean was a particularly expressive oppositional staple for ecological reasons as well ... eastern civilizations discovered early on that soy was well adapted to a society pressed by growing population, limited land, and scarce energy—the very opposite of the American core food, the burger, which took so much land and energy to produce and distribute. (Belasco 1989: 56)

We see, therefore, that vegetarian ideology does not merely reflect the traditional food hierarchy minus meat; rather, it challenges and subverts it. Employing the language of "alive" and "dead" in ways that subvert normal usage by the dominant culture, the paradox of vegetarianism inheres:

> ... thus they do not eat living things and yet we find vegetarians speaking of vegetarian food as "alive" and meat as "dead" (and this deadness is extended also to the deadness of over refined processed foods). The ways in which these oppositions are worked through are complex. Put briefly, however, vegetarianism asserts the existence and importance of a different sort of "power" and "vigour" from that traditionally embodied in meat; the "life" in vegetarian food is closely connected with images of lightness, sunshine and eternal youthfulness in conscious opposition to what is perceived as meat's embodiment of death, decay and corruption, and these opposing qualities underwrite a series of political, aesthetic and moral perceptions. (Twigg 1983: 29)

Ideologically speaking, meat-eating culture inherently involves sexual politics, as scholars have shown, as meat-eating is identified repeatedly with maleness, masculinity, virility, and strength (Twigg 1979, 1983; Adam 1994; Gruin 1994; Martin 1994). The American vernacular terminology of meat-eating reflects this masculine bias (e.g., "a man's meal," "man-sized portions," "hero sandwich," "manhandlers," "meat-and-potatoes men"), and many examples of gendered beliefs exist that posit men needing meat more than women do, or even in some cases of children and pregnant or lactating women cautioned about being too vulnerable to eat the powerful red meat for fear they will be overcome by it (Twigg 1983; Adams 2003). It follows then that meat manifests as a symbol of male dominance, a celebration of patriarchy itself.

In her classic essay, "Deciphering a Meal," Mary Douglas suggests that such details as the order in which food is served, the foods that are expected to be present at a meal, and so on, reflect a "taxonomy of classification that mirrors and reinforces our larger culture." The center of the dominant meat-eating culture's meal, of course, is meat—the standard by which other meals are judged—and the pattern and order of dishes leading up to this main entrée is evidence of cultural and familial stability. Hence, says Douglas (1975: 273), "the strong arousal power of a threat to weaken or confuse that category." A vegetarian's decision to remove meat from her or his individual plate is perceived to be, in this light, threatening to the structure of the larger family system, perhaps to patriarchal culture itself (Adams 1994). As such, Mary McCarthy's *Birds of America* describes an encounter that illustrates how a woman's eschewal of meat is taken by the male host, a NATO general, as a subversive act requiring an aggressive response. The vegetarian's refusal of turkey at the Thanksgiving meal angers the general, "as male dominance requires a continual recollection of itself on everyone's plate" (Adams 1994: 555). In response, the general piles turkey onto her plate and ladles the meat-based gravy over the potatoes as well as the meat, "thus contaminating her vegetable foods." This description of the general's actions with food mirrors the customs associated with military battles, as McCarthy writes, "He had seized the gravy boat like a weapon in hand-to-hand combat" (1971: 196). Although extreme, this example compels us to view meat-eating in families as a form of patriarchal domination that "requires a continual recollection of itself on everyone's plate." In fact, this kind of incident was frequently described in vegetarian personal experience narratives that recount conflicts occurring when vegetarians and meat-eaters "gather together" to eat within the institution of the family meal.

Family Reactions to Vegetarianism

∷

If patriotism is indeed "the love of the good things we ate in our childhood," as Lin Yutang remarks, then it makes sense that vegetarians are initially perceived by their families to be unpatriotic, un-American, and even downright un-family like. Noting the importance of family foodways as a "vehicle for the transmission of the family culture," James Bossard (1943: 297) observed that the family meal "serves constantly as an evaluating conference, especially to the experiences, needs, and interests of family members." Writing of his own experience becoming vegetarian in the 1970s, Belasco (1989: 7) describes the ensuing "family food fights": "within two years, we too were vegetarian ... Back east my sister-in-law Leni was provoking loud dinner table arguments by refusing meat and championing granola; when her younger sister Marty defected too, family dinners became intense indeed." It is largely through the institution of the family meal, in fact, that families express their opinions about the individual's decision to become vegetarian. It follows, then, that anecdotes regarding conflicts during family meals are central to the genre of vegetarian personal experience narratives, usually following their explanation of why they became vegetarian. A study by Jabs et al. (1998a: 186) similarly notes that most of the opposition to vegetarianism comes from family members.

> In general, respondents' nuclear families were not supportive of vegetarian diets. Respondents' parents often attempted to discourage them from adopting a vegetarian diet in their youth. For respondents who adopted a vegetarian diet as adults, their non vegetarian children were often unsupportive of their parents' dietary changes. A 72-year old, pesco-vegetarian relayed her interactions with her "meat eating" daughter at Thanksgiving. "We don't interact too much with them [daughter and her husband] as far as food is concerned ... She said to me 'Are you going to make a turkey?' 'No' I said ... 'Oh well, then we're not coming.' That was very hurtful."

Conflicts ensue not just because the change poses logistical challenges (for example in terms of what the vegetarian will eat), but also because the change is initially perceived as a challenge to established food traditions. Because of the close connection between food and identity—as in the well-worn adage "we are what we eat"—and because the sharing of food enables the family to maintain communitas, does *refusing* to eat some symbolically laden food item affect one's ability to belong to that family? It would appear that this very question is a part of what is negotiated via these conflicts and is the root of why, in some cases, the change is taken to be a threat to family foodways and hence a threat to familial identity itself.

While the reactions of families to each individual vegetarian vary in tone and degree, they seem to parallel each other in several ways. The vegetarians who shared their stories with me described their families reacting in a number of ways, which I have tried to group together conceptually into seven categories. Obviously, however, some of these reactions bleed over into more than one category.

1. TREATING THE CHANGE AS "JUST A PHASE"

First, family members dismissed the vegetarian's decision as "just a phase," which possibly suggests wishful thinking as well as an intuitive understanding that changing food behaviors "goes with" changing lifestyles (see Jabs *et al.* 1998). Scott recounts:

> I'd told my family about it and they were like, "Yeah, whatever." And I remember my mom saying at dinner one night to my younger brother, "Are you going to eat that chicken, it's good for you?" And I was like, "Who told you that, Mom?" And she started yelling at me about how, "blah, blah, blah," and I said something to my dad, and he yelled back, "I eat meat because I LIKE IT!" (Interview, October 2002)

This attitude of the change only being temporary can function in some instances as a form of denial, allowing the family to not worry excessively about the change or its consequences. In other cases, though, this response was intended to allow the phase to pass quietly and quickly, as in Dan's case:

> Well, my family thought I was weird anyway, before that. They just thought this was just another weird thing. But they assumed it was just temporary. It would pass. And they didn't make any effort to cook anything different.
>
> Well, that's their attitude toward my eccentricities in general, you know, "Whatever ..." ... My mom just thought I was, you know, a crazy teenager going through a phase, and it would pass. And the least big a deal they made of it [laughs], the faster it would probably pass. (Interview, September 2002)

Because vegetarianism presents an "explicit food ideology," it can be used to look at the ideology of the dominant meat culture, which is more pervasive and implicit. Everything being vegetarian represents has its opposite in the midwestern agricultural communities, in the attitudes, beliefs, and traditions surrounding the self-proclaimed "meat and potatoes people." Vegetarian ideology exists within the context of meat-eating ideology, a fact revealed via billboards that stretch across the highways of the Midwest that could be taken as a warning to potential vegetarian visitors: "Beef. It's what's for dinner." Twigg suggests that "The Western ... vegetarian is very much a product of individual choice, and indeed, requiring one, as it does, to step outside the culturally prescribed forms of eating, depending on the development of a highly individuated sense of the self" (Twigg 1983: 19). Adolescence, explain Michael Nichols and Richard Schwartz (1998: 151), "is a time when children no longer want to be like Mommy and Daddy; they want to be themselves. They struggle to become autonomous individuals, and they struggle to open family boundaries." In a similar vein, John Leo (1979: 112) argues that American youth who become vegetarian represent an example of how food can be employed to act out generational battles. Belasco likewise suggests that

> The high that came with breaking food conventions stemmed in part from the shock value. As many neovegetarians discovered when they first requested alfalfa sprouts and chopsticks over roast beef and stainless steel, the countercuisine brought the [Vietnam] war home to the family dinner table. At first parents and friends might easily dismiss the defection as adolescent perversity—a predictably familiar desire to be different. (Belasco 1989: 28; see also 179)

Perhaps the decision to become vegetarian, therefore, reveals early power struggles with authority. Indeed, most of my interviewees were teenagers (or just beyond) when they made their decisions; and with the advantage of hindsight, many cited a desire for independence as part of their reasoning although, at the time, this seem unrelated to them. When Howard informed his family of his decision to become vegetarian, he says, "My parents sort of chuckled. They thought I was being faddish." Similarly, Christina said that looking back on her decision now, nearly two decades later, "It was kinda, I think, an independence thing … an attempt to separate myself. And, yeah, I think it worked. I mean, I think I felt like, 'Yeah, I'm a vegetarian!' you know, 'I'm different'" (Interview, September 2002).[7] Also present in the family's reaction of treating it as a phase is awareness on the part of family members that vegetarianism accompanies other significant life transitions (see Jabs *et al.* 1998).

2. ATTEMPTING TO PRESSURE, PERSUADE, TEMPT OR TRICK THE VEGETARIAN INTO EATING MEAT

While family members articulated concern about nutritional needs, vegetarians perceived that family members often tried to pressure or persuade them to eat meat. There are numerous examples of these kinds of responses from the vegetarians I interviewed; they seem, in fact, to be an important part of the story. The younger sister of one vegetarian whose father was a cattle farmer pleaded with her to "at least eat it around Dad," to avoid offending him (Interview, September 1996). Michael's mother, for nearly ten years, kept "badgering" him to "Eat some … just a little … eat just a … eat a piece of fish … eat something … it's not going to hurt you," claiming she feared he was "going to get sick and die." And his father would periodically encourage him to eat some fish by saying, "It's alright. You can go off the wagon now and then" (Interview, September 2002).[8] Similarly, at a family wedding, Beth's extended family pressured her to give up being vegetarian.

> And I remember becoming really frustrated because at every meal, while I was eating, people would question me about why I don't eat meat and this and that. I mean, people did that at every meal this summer. Whether it was an aunt or a cousin, they would get on my case, "Really, you should eat meat." "You're really not getting all your recommended nutrition." "You really need to eat meat." And at every meal, I was just getting so frustrated because I would just want to eat and they'd be just watching what I put on my plate, what I'm eating, and just drill me about it. I would get so mad at them! (Interview, October 2002)

Likewise, Cora's family tried to change her mind on the basis of nutrition:

> I never really declared myself vegetarian to my family. It was more that my eating patterns changed over time. And their reaction was more like, "Do you have an eating disorder?" As opposed to, "Are you now a vegetarian?" Just because I was becoming more concerned with healthy eating in general. My family eats really unhealthfully; they just don't like anything healthy. So they kinda reacted negatively just because they're like, all of a sudden I was eating all this healthy stuff! [laughs]. (Interview, October 2002)

Beth found that her family also tried to "tempt" her to eat meat, even seven years later: "Still, every once in a while, my mother will try to tempt me with something I used to really like (e.g., teriyaki chicken). 'Are you *sure*, you used to like this?' But I think she was mostly concerned about my health." And sometimes they even tried to "trick" her into doing so:

> My family would try to trick me into eating meat. For example, they'd cut it into little pieces, tell me it's something else, just to gross me out. Or once my brother put a big piece of bacon on top of my food because he wanted to see if I would still eat it, after the bacon had touched it. It was a really immature thing, but for some reason, they really got a kick out of like grossing me out with the meat or telling me there's not meat in something and trying to get me to eat it. I don't really understand the pleasure in that. (Interview, October 2002)

3. CHALLENGING THE LOGICAL/PHILOSOPHICAL BASIS OF THE CHOICE

It seems that from the moment their decision is made known, the vegetarian individual finds her or himself repeatedly bombarded with questions from friends and family. Howard's Catholic family was first exposed to his decision at Christmas time. "My parents sort of chuckled. They thought I was being faddish," Howard says. When Howard refused to eat fish, "The conversation stopped." "Fish isn't meat," his cousin challenged, to which Howard retorted that fish were once alive. "We haven't gotten along ever since!" Howard jokes, "But I never really liked her that much anyway" (Interview, May 1995). Belasco (1989: 60–61) likewise observes this phenomenon, recounting some of these philosophical challenges to vegetarians:

> As for the humanitarian argument against flesh, wasn't it murder to eat a seed before it sprouted, to pull weeds or kill bugs that through no fault of theirs interfered with your own predatory needs or social conventions? Wasn't it inherently imperialistic to tame vegetable species? Were those who kept animals for dairy products so free from blame? Wasn't the domestication of animals similar to the subjugation of women in households? How could a vegetarian support abortion?

In fact, sometimes they are challenged so successfully on logical or philosophical grounds that it seems necessary to formulate a more "logical justification." If they still consume some animal products (i.e., wearing leather shoes) or eat other things like Jell-O and Twinkies (which contain gelatin, made of horse hooves), these behavioral inconsistencies were enthusiastically pointed out to the vegetarian. According to several of the vegetarians with whom I spoke, because they could not justify or understand their own contradictory behaviors and beliefs, they either tried to adjust their behavior or, for example, avoid "morality" as an answer to the question of why they do not eat meat, creating cognitive consistency, "the desire of people to reduce dissonance and find agreement between existing beliefs and values and new information" (Jabs *et al.* 1998b: 196).

4. ANGER AND ACCUSING THE VEGETARIAN OF BETRAYING FAMILY VALUES

Especially if the eschewal of meat conflicts with traditional beliefs and practices (e.g., that fish is not really meat), the vegetarian's behavior is viewed as deviant and threatening, perhaps even a betrayal to the family identity itself. "In general," according to one study, "the symbolic foods of holidays, such as turkey and lamb, were sources of tension between vegetarians and non-vegetarian family members. Non-vegetarian family members often decreased their social interactions with respondents due to them following a vegetarian diet" (Jabs *et al.* 1998a: 186). One interviewee, who had been beginning to adopt a vegetarian diet, abandoned the cause for fear of his family's reaction:

It began in graduate school. I hadn't been eating very much meat ... At the time, I realized that I didn't like ham at all. When I went to my family's house for a meal, I said before the meal, "I don't want ham. I don't eat ham." And my dad got really mad and made a really big deal about it, saying, "Oh, you don't eat ham now, huh? Now you're a vegetarian, huh?" He made jokes about it at times; at other times, he'd get upset about it. Of course, I was thinking about becoming a vegetarian, but I didn't want to deal with my family's reaction every time we ate ribs, barbeque, and stuff. And I also didn't want to feel excluded from my family's traditions. I couldn't even imagine myself going home for Thanksgiving and not eating turkey. They wouldn't even understand if I didn't. (Interview, October 2002)

In a similar vein, Cora explained, "Like for Christmas dinner, we had like nothing really good for you [laughs], and so I would eat the stuff [meat] just to like ... not cause conflict at the table. Because I don't want to be like, 'I don't like Christmas dinner,' you know" (Interview, October 2002). On the other hand, Scott finds that sometimes holiday meals are easier times to be vegetarian because there are more food options than at non-holiday meals: "Like at Thanksgiving, for example, I don't need to eat it [meat] because there are tons of other side dishes" (Interview, September 2002).

Family systems theory can be usefully employed here to understand the reactions of families towards the vegetarian. Nichols and Schwartz (1998: 244) explain that, "Family structure involves a set of covert rules that govern transactions in the family ... [a rule] will be manifested in various ways depending on the context and which family members are involved ... but altering the basic structure will have ripple effects on all family transactions ... Whatever the chosen pattern, it tends to be self-perpetuating and resistant to change." Many theorists like to think of families as systems trying to maintain equilibrium, characterizing them as "rule-governed homeostatic systems" (Nichols and Schwartz 1998: 90). The concept of "homeostasis" refers to the tendency of systems to self-regulate to maintain cohesion in response to changes in the environment. Coined by French physiologist Claude Bernard in the nineteenth century to describe the regulation of such bodily conditions as temperature and blood sugar levels, the term is useful in the modern context to describe the tendency of families to resist change (Nichols and Schwartz 1998: 114). Some theorists have suggested the counter term "morphogenesis" (e.g., Speer 1970) to account for the individual's desire to seek, in addition to resisting, change. The vegetarian's decision manifests basically as a disruption or reversal of the "family script"—the continuity of family values, practices, beliefs—which supports Paul Thompson's assertion that, "influence can be handed down [by families] either through imitation *or through rejection* of a previous generation's pattern" (Thompson 1993: 32–33; emphasis added).

In folkloristic parlance, the "reversal" of the family script can be seen as "innovation," while the process of family systems resisting change is often referred to as the constant negotiation between innovation and tradition (e.g., Georges and Jones 1995), between conservatism and dynamism (e.g., Schoemaker 1990), or sometimes, "like the Sisyphus myth, the rock is pushed up the hill, but then it is rolled partially back down again" (Baraka 1994: 5). Thus, although the vegetarians I interviewed emphasized to their families that their decision resulted from personal reasons (e.g., usually taste), and although most avoided trying to persuade other members of the family to stop eating meat, somehow their families inherently understood that being vegetarian "goes with" much more than simply not eating meat, that food choices represent a broader system of ideologies than the immediate challenge of finding alternative food options at family meals.

In fact, the non-food changes many of these vegetarians enacted (e.g., going to college, changing dress and hair styles, experimenting with alcohol/drugs, sexual activity, religious orientation, and so forth) were not mutually exclusive but rather they were interrelated, as Twigg suggests. Their highly politicized alternative social values—suggesting alternative visions of the dominant culture's social structures, institutions, and relationships—were symbolized by their choice to become vegetarian. Because these values, however, undermine familial structures that embrace the dominant culture's conventional ways of thinking and doing things, in effect their vegetarianism represents radical, subversive ideology to their families. The families recognize this dynamic process of changing identity and ideology through food choice and resist the ripples of changes created within the homeostasis of their system, which "threatened to destroy that which was traditional and meaningful in the old life" (Gutierrez 1984: 171).

The common family reactions discussed above demonstrate resistance to what is initially perceived as a threat to a traditional way of life. On one level families know the vegetarian is resisting more than just meat; they are resisting an entire "outsider" ideology that they understand to accompany it. Hence, many of their behaviors are intended to effect a change in the family member's food behaviors, in hopes of returning the family's foodways—and the family itself—back to its homeostatic condition; or in folkloristic terms, to resist the attempted innovation on the family's established food tradition.

5. MAKING CONCILIATORY GESTURES AND AVOIDING CONFLICT

As seen above, many vegetarians are willing to eat some meat, especially items symbolically connected to holidays, to avoid generating conflict with the family and to continue to feel they are still a valid part of the family. Additionally, most avoid going into detail about exactly why they chose to eschew meat with their meat-eating families. Simple statements such as, "I don't eat meat" or "I'm vegetarian," might be all they offer as an explantion, as if not eating meat were no less symbolically charged than saying, for example, "I don't eat chocolate." Their efforts at downplaying the meaning of their status in front of meat-eating family members reveals something interesting—that in spite of the need to assert their independence there is a concurrent desire to avoid conflict and to avoid the appearance that they're lecturing to their family, or otherwise making them "feel guilty" by remarks about eating meat being "gross" or "morally wrong." Around other vegetarians, however, they are much more explicit in their explanations. On this note, some food scholars have pointed out that meat's ability to provoke unease, a phenomenon typically not found in vegetable-based foods, may reveal "an underlying unease, even guilt, within the dominant culture over meat-eating evidenced in myths and legends" (Twigg 1983: 22; see also Adams 2003). And vegetarians have also remarked that the reason meat "'has' to be cooked is precisely to disguise its bloody taste, hide its true nature. Meat can be stomached [by most] because in the process of cooking the 'power' in meat is to some extent tamed ..." (Twigg 1983: 25). This alleged phenomenon of guilt might shed light on why several vegetarians referred to their "relapse" from vegetarianism as a "fall from grace," referencing the Edenic myth of the Garden of Eden where Adam and Eve are depicted as having been vegetarians.

In spite of the possibility of underlying guilt, a number of my informants report that on rare occasions they ate meat to avoid offending a host, who, unaware of the vegetarian's diet, had prepared meat dishes for them. Christina recalls:

> This was when I was a sophomore or junior in high school. I was a guest at someone's grandmother's house, and I was too embarrassed to say anything about it [being vegetarian]. And they served steak, of all things. And I took maybe two bites of it, to be polite. And I felt physically ill the rest of the night. I mean, I was literally ... I had a tummy ache. [laughs] I mean, I was disgusted—physically and mentally. And so that taught me a lesson. I thought, I'll never eat meat again ... ever. (Interview, September 2002)

Beth recalls that once, early into her vegetarianism, she was at a boyfriend's parent's house for dinner. "And his father cooked pork chops, of all things, on the rib. And I ate it. I hadn't been away from it for very long. But I remember the family ... they were intimidating parents, so there was no way I could have been like, 'I'm sorry, I can't eat that.' And I had to bite it off the rib and it was disgusting. It was horrible!" (Interview, October 2002). Similarly, Michael, an otherwise very strict vegetarian, recounts:

> There's another story that comes to mind. I went to Korea for a few weeks as part of my work. And I went to a family's home for a night. And the person who organized the home visits knew the family whose house I was going to, and she knew I was vegetarian, and she said she would tell them that I was vegetarian. Well, I got there and they started bringing out all these meat dishes, just one after the next, and the next. And it was obvious that she hadn't told them. So I ate it, you know, I just figured I'm not going to insult these people. I just didn't feel strongly enough, I guess, in my conviction … I don't know what it was, but I just decided to eat it. And then later, I saw the woman who'd organized the trip, and she said, "Oh, how was your dinner?" And I just said, "Oh, it was fine," I didn't want to say anything … but then she said, "Oh, good. I didn't tell them you were vegetarian, since there are so many vegetables in Korean cooking, anyway." [laughs] But they [the family] made a special attempt … because we were Americans, you know, they thought we had to have a lot of meat, so they did away with all the traditional vegetables and they served us a lot of meat. (Interview, September 2002)

In these cases, which are common, the vegetarian's desire to avoid social conflict or offending the host and to have a social communion with the host is so powerful that it overrides the decision to not eat meat and yet is perceived by the vegetarian in some cases as a sign of weakness—"I just didn't feel strongly enough, I guess, in my conviction." This willingness, even of strict vegetarians, to make "an exception" tends to occur, significantly, more often in meals of which the vegetarian is not a family member.

Undoubtedly, either the family or the vegetarian (or both) eventually adapt, family members make accommodating gestures, and the frequency and intensity of conflicts decreases. Recalling how he gradually began to make exceptions for the sake of some family meals, Scott noted that

> Now that I've matured, though, what I want to communicate to my family when I'm with them is that there is a communal sense and that they feel love coming from me, not that I'm just putting in their faces that what they do [eating meat] is wrong in my eyes. So I avoid making a big deal about it now. (Interview, September 2002)

Beth, who makes no exceptions to her own vegetarian practice, recalls a transformation with her mother: "Now she'll make tofu or polenta. She's been interested in trying new things. She now understands that I can't *just* eat steamed veggies, that I need protein and stuff too. She'll come home from the store with all sorts of things for me to eat."

The lack of extensive commentary in vegetarian personal experience narratives about efforts their families made to accommodate their changed diet might give the impression that the family is always adversarial toward the vegetarian. This is not the case, however; when asked pointedly, many of the interviewees reported their family making conciliatory gestures of some sort after a period of time. These gestures sometimes simply included fewer instances of arguing or challenging the vegetarian's behavior, acquiring non-meat protein alternatives at family meals, inviting the vegetarian herself or himself to cook a dish for the meal, and so forth. The fact that this dynamic is routinely absent from the vegetarian narratives I collected, unless the vegetarians were specifically asked about it, however, suggests to me that the personal experience narratives are designed largely to account for the etiology of the decision to refuse meat and to cope with the stress of ensuing conflicts by talking about their more painful experiences, perhaps creating their own sense of communitas, even, with other vegetarians via such storytelling sessions.

Conclusion

Comparing these kinds of vegetarian personal experience narratives proves fruitful in beginning to understand the dynamic transformations in behavior, thought, emotion, philosophy, and taste that tend to occur when individuals decide to resist the dominant meat culture by becoming vegetarian. Vegetarianism manifests as an explicit ideology, subverting the values and beliefs expressed via the dominant meat-eating culture's implicit ideology, and this is crucial to understanding these intrafamilial conflicts.

How families with traditional meat-centered diets respond to vegetarian ideals, however, also reveals a great deal about family psychosocial dynamics. Family systems theory illuminates these strong reactions, in which the family resists the vegetarian's new role, exhibiting contradictory impulses toward the "deviant" family member and attempting to maintain the family's homeostasis as manifested through its foodways. As such, vegetarianism, like other major life changes, disrupts the status quo of the family structure at a very emotionally laden point—its food traditions. Considering food behavior in this way forges promising new directions for further research into the interrelationship among food behavior, family foodways, family and individual identity, and family relational dynamics in ways that move beyond celebratory depictions of familial meal traditions, toward a theory of how food behavior and ideology also work to negotiate power, belonging, and exclusion.

Notes

1 See, for example, Chappelle (1972); Graham (1981); Georges (1984); Humphrey and Humphrey (1988); Turner and Seriff (1993); Shuman (2001).

2 Some exceptions to the celebratory approach to foodways that come to mind include Bordo (1997); Adams (1998); hooks (1998); Witt (1998); Heldke (2001); Schell (2001).

3 For work on how diet is linked to ideologies of class, ethnicity, and gender, see Turner (1987); Levenstein (1988); Fiddes (1991); and Inness (2002).

4 I spoke informally with roughly forty current and former vegetarians and conducted in-depth, open-ended, semi-structured, tape-recorded interviews with thirty, recruited via snowball sampling. Of these, 85% were European American, the remaining 15% claiming African-American, Japanese-American, and Jewish-American ethnicities. Ages ranged from twenty-two to forty-two years of age, 75% being female, 25% male. All were well-educated and reported being middle class. They varied in terms of both duration and kind of vegetarianism practiced. A few of my interviewees were residents of California but most were currently living in Missouri. In the case of the California group, their families hailed from other states (e.g., Florida, New York, Virginia). For the most part, therefore, my data set is weighted towards Caucasian, middle-class, Midwestern Americans. In light of these limitations, this study should be viewed as suggestive, rather than generalizable to all American vegetarians and their families. Differing geographical regions, ethnicities, age, class, and so forth, might produce different results. In addition to the interviews, I observed how this issue manifests in popular American culture (for example, via film, literature, cartoons, and so forth) for further insights. It is important to note that I did not interview the families of vegetarians, but only the vegetarians themselves. One would expect family members to present a different point of view and different versions of the narratives—an issue left unexplored here.

5 This motivation for becoming vegetarian is revealed in Dan's case:

> When I was in eleventh grade, I read the book *Diet for a Small Planet*. And the book made an argument that the beef industry and the meat industry of the U.S. was ecologically unsound, and that all of the grazing land and grain that was used for raising animals for meat, could be better used for raising food to feed people. And that the problem of world hunger would be solved more quickly simply by not raising animals for food. So I started trying to be a vegetarian after I read that book, because that argument made perfect sense to me.

We see how this story of how/why he became a vegetarian moves quickly from ecological and political considerations to the more spiritual, for in the very next sentence he adds the explanation:

> The other thing was that I grew up where I saw animals slaughtered, you know, butchered for meat. So between the two things—just the humanitarian idea of, "wouldn't it be nice if we didn't have to kill these animals?" and the ecological part of it … that's really why I decided to be vegetarian … I just don't think it's right to eat blood. Animals eat blood. In my mind, on some level, I guess I'm making it moral: human beings don't eat blood; animals eat blood. I know people do really eat blood [laughs], but it just seems like you shouldn't. (Interview, September 2002)

6 As a matter of fact, five of my female interviewees mentioned that, considering most meat was "gross" to them anyway, their motivation to eliminate all meat was influenced by the desire to lose weight. Following a "gross-out" experience, therefore, becoming vegetarian seemed to be a convenient technique for weight control (see Bordo 1997). "I'll say it was probably for all the wrong reasons," explained Cora, "because it was connected to my concern about my weight." Likewise, Beth said "Because of my eating problems, it [vegetarianism] was a good excuse." And Christina added in hindsight that, "I also think it may have been an attempt for me to control my diet, for weight reasons."

7 If becoming vegetarian manifests as a form of protest against parental food norms, it is intriguing to ponder how the children of vegetarians might rebel. Consider Belasco's (1989: 247) description of his own family:

> Like most parents nowadays, both my wife and I work full-time. Although we've found quick vegetarian recipes for ourselves, we still don't know what to serve our seven-year-old, who hates beans and bulgur, barely tolerates tofu, but loves fish sticks, McNuggets, and fries; once he gets molars, our toddler will no doubt side with her.

Belasco happily reported as an update that "My kids turned out well … they eat very little meat—so we didn't have the vegetarian backlash I initially feared" (e-mail communication, February 22, 2005).

8 Borrowing language from alcohol/drug recovery programs to describe this food behavior is intriguing; it seems that both vegetarians and their families use this kind of language. Many vegetarians repeatedly make reference to themselves and others being "addicted" to meat. Michael, however, vehemently protested his father's use of the term ("he said it as if I were *addicted* to meat"), whereas Christi reports that she only "relapsed once" on a McDonald's chicken sandwich, Christina had "one lapse," and Howard reports he "went cold turkey" off of meat but now describes himself as a "lapsed vegetarian."

References
: :
ADAMS, C. J. 1994. The Sexual Politics of Meat. In A. M. Jaggar (ed) *Living with Contradictions: Controversies in Feminist Social Ethnics*, pp. 548–557. Boulder, CO: Westview Press.
———. [1990] 2003. *The Sexual Politics of Meat: A Feminist-Vegetarian Critical Theory*. New York: Continuum.
ANGYAL, A. 1941. Disgust and Related Aversions. *Journal of Abnormal and Social Psychology* 36: 393–412.
BABCOCK, C. 1948. Food and Its Emotional Significance. *American Dietetic Association Journal* 24(5): 390–393.
BARAKA, A. 1994. Cultural Revolution and the Canon. In A. Waldman and A. Schelling (eds) *Disembodied Poetics: Annals of the Jack Kerouac School*, pp. 22–32. Albuquerque, NM: University of New Mexico Press.
BARTHES, R. [1961] 1997. Toward a Psychosociology of Contemporary Food Consumption. In C. Counihan and P. Van Esterik (eds) *Food and Culture: A Reader*, pp. 20–7. New York: Routledge.
BEARDSWORTH, A. D. and KEIL, E. T. 1991. Health-Related Beliefs and Dietary Practices among Vegetarians and Vegans: A Qualitative Study. *Health Education Journal* 50: 38–42.
BELASCO, W. J. 1989. *Appetite for Change: How the Counterculture Took on the Food Industry, 1966–1988*. New York: Pantheon Books.
BORDO, S. 1997. Anorexia Nervosa: Psychopathology as the Crystallization of Culture. In C. Counihan and P. Van Esterik (eds) *Food and Culture: A Reader*, pp. 226-250. New York: Routledge.
BOSSARD, J. H. 1943. Family Table Talk—An Area for Sociological Study. *American Sociological Review* 18: 295–301.
DOUGLAS, M. 1966. *Purity and Danger: An Analysis of the Concepts of Pollution and Taboo*. London: Routledge.
———. 1975. Deciphering a Meal. In M. Douglas (ed) *Implicit Meanings: Essays in Anthropology*. London: Routledge & Kegan Paul.
FARB, P. and ARMELAGOS, G. 1980. *Consuming Passions: The Anthropology of Eating*, pp. 197–226. Boston, MA: Houghton Mifflin.
FIDDES, N. 1991. *Meat: A Natural Symbol*. London: Routledge.
GEORGES, R. A. 1984. You Often Eat What Others Think You Are: Food As An Index of Others' Conceptions of Who One Is. *Western Folklore* 43(4): 246–253.
GEORGES, R. A. and JONES, M. O. 1995. *Folkloristics: An Introduction*. Bloomington, IN: Indiana University Press.
GRAHAM, A. 1981. "Let's Eat!" Commitment and Communion in Cooperative Households. *Western Folklore* 40: 55–63.
GRUIN, L. 1994. Dismantling Oppression: An Analysis of the Connection between Women and Animals. In Jaggar, A. M. *Living with Contradictions: Controversies in Feminist Social Ethics*, pp. 537–548. Boulder, CO: Westview Press.
GUTIERREZ, C. P. 1984. The Social and Symbolic Uses of Ethnic/Regional Foodways: Cajuns and Crawfish in South Louisiana. In Brown, L. and Mussell, K. (eds) *Ethnic and Regional Foodways in the United States*, pp. 169–182. Knoxville, TN: University of Tennessee Press.
HELDKE, L. 2001. Let's Cook Thai: Recipes for Colonialism. In S. A. Inness (ed) *Pilaf, Pozole, and Pad Thai: American Women and Ethnic Foods*, pp. 175–197. Amherst, MA: University of Massachusetts Press.

HOOKS, B. 1998. Eating the Other: Desire and Resistance. In R. Scapp and B. Seitz (eds) *Eating Culture*, pp. 181–200. Albany, NY: State University of New York Press.

HUMPHREY, T. C. and HUMPHREY, L. T. (eds) 1988. *"We Gather Together": Food and Festival in American Life*, pp. 19–26. Ann Arbor, MI: UMI Research Press.

INNESS, S. A. (ed). 2001. *Kitchen Culture in America: Popular Representations of Food, Gender, and Race*. Philadelphia, PA: University of Pennsylvania Press.

JABS, J., DEVINE, C. M. and SOBAL, J. 1998a. Maintaining Vegetarian Diets: Personal Factors, Social Networks and Environmental Resources. *Canadian Journal of Dietetic Practice and Research* 59(4): 183–188.

——— . 1998b. Model of the Process of Adopting Vegetarian Diets: Health Vegetarians and Ethical Vegetarians. *Journal of Nutrition Education* 30(4): 196–202.

KALČIK, S. 1984. Ethnic Foodways in America: Symbol and the Performance of Identity. L. Keller Brown and K. Mussell (eds) *Ethnic and Regional Foodways in the United States: The Performance of Group Identity*, pp. 37–65. Knoxville, TN: The University of Tennessee Press.

KRISTEVA, J. 1982. *Powers of Horror: An Essay on Abjection*. Trans. Roudiez, L. S. New York: Columbia University Press.

LAPPÉ, F. M. 1971. *Diet for a Small Planet*. New York: Ballantine Books.

LEO, J. 1979. How to Beat the Beef Against Meat. *Time* (November 5): 112.

LEVENSTEIN, H. 1988. *Revolution at the Table: The Transformation of the American Diet*. New York: Oxford University Press.

MARTIN, L. 1994. Feminism and Vegetarianism. In A. M. Jaggar (ed) *Living with Contradictions: Controversies in Feminist Social Ethnics*, pp. 557–560. Boulder, CO: Westview Press.

MCCARTHY, M. 1971. *Birds of America*. New York: Harcourt Brace Jovanovich.

NEWTON, S. E. 1992. The Jell-O Syndrome: Investigating Popular Culture/Foodways. *Western Folklore* 51: 249–267.

NICHOLS, M. P. and SCHWARTZ, R. C. [1984] 1998. *Family Therapy: Concepts and Methods*. Boston, MA: Allyn & Bacon.

PALMERINO, C. C. 1981. Pleasing the Palate: Diet Selection and Aversion Learning. *Western Folklore* 40: 19–27.

SCHELL, H. 2001. Gendered Feasts: A Feminist Reflects on Dining in New Orleans. In S. A. Inness (ed) *Pilaf, Pozole, and Pad Thai: American Women and Ethnic Food*, pp. 199–221. Amherst, MA: University of Massachusetts Press.

SCHOEMAKER, G. H. 1990. *The Emergence of Folklore in Everyday Life: A Fieldguide and Sourcebook*, pp. 1–10. Bloomington, IN: Trickster Press.

SHUMAN, A. 2001. Food Gifts: Ritual Exchange and the Production of Excess Meaning. *Journal of American Folklore* 113(450): 495–508.

THOMPSON, P. 1993. Family Myth, Models, and Denials in the Shaping of Individual Life Paths. In D. Bertaux and P. Thompson (eds) *Between Generations: Family Models, Myths, and Memories*, pp. 13–38. Oxford: Oxford University Press.

TURNER, K. and SERIF, S. 1993. "Giving an Altar to St. Joseph": A Feminist Perspective on a Patronal Feast. In S. Tower Hollis, L. Pershing and M. J. Young (eds) *Feminist Theory and the Study of Folklore*, pp. 89–117. Urbana: University of Illinois Press.

TURNER, P. A. 1987. Church's Fried Chicken and The Klan: A Rhetorical Analysis of Rumor in the Black Community. *Western Folklore* 46: 294–306.

TWIGG, J. 1979. Food for Thought: Purity and Vegetarianism. *Religion* 9(Spring): 13–35.

——— . 1983. Vegetarianism and the Meanings of Meat. In A. Murcott (ed) *The Sociology of Food and Eating: Essays on the Sociological Significance of Food*. London: Gower.

VOLLMECKE, R. P. 1986. Food Likes and Dislikes. *Annual Review of Nutrition* 6: 433–456.

WITT, D. 1998. Soul Food: Where the Chitterling Hits the (Primal) Pan. In. R. Scapp and B. Seitz (eds) *Eating Culture*, pp. 258–87. Albany, NY: State University of New York Press.

ZEITLIN, S. J. 1980. An Alchemy of Mind: The Family Courtship Story. *Western Folklore* 39: 17–33.

Carole **Counihan**
Millersville University

··Food, Feelings and Film

WOMEN'S POWER IN *LIKE WATER FOR CHOCOLATE*

This paper uses the Mexican film *Like Water for Chocolate* (1991) to address the question of how women can use food as a path to power. Directed by Alfonso Arau based on his wife Laura Esquivel's screenplay, the film uses lush and sensual images of foods and cooking to articulate a rich picture of family and gender. By portraying several characters' relationship to food, and through food to each other, the film suggests multiple ways women can carve out diversely empowering or demeaning roles.

::

In this paper,[1] I address the question of whether women can transform cooking, feeding, and eating from sites of oppression into sources of power. I use as a text the Mexican film *Como agua para chocolate / Like Water for Chocolate* (1991) directed by Alfonso Arau from his wife Laura Esquivel's (1989) novel and screenplay. Food is a central focus and symbol in the film. The many close-up shots of food being prepared, served, and eaten emphasize its social and symbolic centrality. Food is particularly important in the film as a voice for women and their abundant emotions and there are many scenes of cooking and eating. I will discuss how the four main female characters—the protagonist Tita; her mother, Mama Elena; and her two sisters, Rosaura and Gertrudis—relate differently to food. I will also look at two principal male characters in the film—the Mexican Pedro, the object of Tita's passion, and the Anglo doctor John Brown, who loves her in vain. Finally, I will also look at how the film defines the relationships of the Indian servants Nacha and Chencha to food, and those of the two Anglo women in the film: John's aunt and his housekeeper, Sue Ellen. I suggest that in these different relationships the film posits answers to the question of how women can gain power through food.

This is a complex question, because cooking and feeding so often involve servitude, drudgery, and compulsion for women, especially women of lower classes and marginalized ethnic groups (Friedlander 1978). Doris Witt (1999), for example, examined the long-standing association of Black women with food in the US epitomized in the Quaker Oats figure of Aunt Jemima. Quaker Oats exploited a stereotypical portrayal of a smiling, plump, Black mammy on the cover of its pancake mix to sell billions of boxes. This image has been part of US cultural casting of Black women as "natural" cooks and servants whose place is in the kitchen ministering to the needs of men and whites.

Rhian Ellis (1983) found that men's dissatisfaction with their wives' cooking was sometimes used as a justification for domestic violence. Similarly, in her study of diverse women in and around the city of Chicago, Marjorie DeVault (1991) found that expectations that women serve husbands and defer to their food preferences reproduced women's subordination and justified their abuse by men. Many of her female subjects felt resentful about their food chores, which involved constant intellectual and physical labor in planning, shopping, cooking, and cleaning up meals—labor about which they had little choice and for which they received little recognition. For many women, being forced to cook, feed, and serve others has been an enactment and symbol of their powerlessness and low status.

Paradoxically, cooking can also be a wellspring of creativity and power for women in diverse ways. For example, in Florence, Italy, in spite of the increasing demands of childcare and work outside the home in the early 1980s, women clung to cooking because creating delicious dishes for husbands and children brought them respect. Being the principal nurturers on whom others depended for emotional as well as physical sustenance gave women influence, especially over children. Yet in 2003, there was increasing evidence that young women were increasingly prioritizing monetary power and workplace jobs over cooking and housework. They were making increasing use of supermarkets, delicatessens, fast food, takeout food, and restaurants, and relinquishing willingly the ambiguous power of cooking (Counihan 1999, 2004).

Women in eighteenth-century Mexico used food directly as a source of power by ensorceling their husbands' food with bits of menstrual blood or water with which they had washed after having sex (Behar 1989). "Typically, women made men 'eat' their witchcraft, using their power over the domain of food preparation for subversive ends" (Behar 1989: 180). Ingestion was a direct and powerful means of influence for, "in eating, the pollution was introduced directly and effectively into the body" (Behar 1989: 180). They were able to stop their husbands' abusive behavior by using food magic to "tie them up" so they were unable to strike their wives. "The belief that food could be used to harm rather than to nurture gave women a very specific and real power that could serve as an important defense against abusive male dominance" (Behar 1989: 180). Similarly, even today in the San Luis Valley of Colorado, villagers believe that witches use food to infect others with their ill-intended wishes (Counihan 2003).

The contrasting positive and negative, good and evil meanings of cooking are at the heart of the film *Like Water for Chocolate*.[2] It centers on women's oft-ignored experiences in the domestic sphere, especially in the kitchen. Although the protagonist Tita is condemned by her mother to a life of servitude, and her role as cook marks her subordinate status in the family, she is able to overcome her subjugation by injecting powerful emotions into her culinary creations which she uses to nurture good and destroy evil.

The movie begins and ends in the modern kitchen of Tita's great niece, the film's narrator. She is chopping an onion and crying, acts that mark her connection to Tita who also always cried when slicing onions. The narrator is reading from Tita's recipe book, her only surviving relic. This scene encapsulates several of the film's major themes: that food is a voice for women, that feeding is powerful when filled with emotions, and that food is an important repository of female traditions that are critical to cultural survival.³

Most of the film takes place in the past with a short first scene in 1895, a long middle scene starting in 1910 in the midst of the Mexican Revolution, and a final short scene in 1934. Tita is the youngest of three daughters of Mama Elena, whose husband dies of a heart attack right after Tita's birth upon hearing that he has been cuckolded. Mama Elena immediately asserts despotic power in the family and decrees that Tita will never marry but must follow family tradition and serve her until she dies. She banishes Tita to the kitchen, like Cinderella (Valdés 1995: 80–81; Zapata 1997: 209), and forbids her from marrying the handsome Pedro with whom she shares passionate love. Mama Elena tries to subordinate Tita's autonomous will by cruel repression in the kitchen, but Tita fights back with food.

In an interview with Claudia Lowenstein (1994), Esquivel talks about how the different relationships of the four central women to food communicate different ways women define themselves and struggle against subordination. Mama Elena adopts a patriarchal stance towards the kitchen; like men she does not cook but rather compels others to cook for her. She is shown cooking only in the very beginning of the movie when she is chopping onions at the kitchen table. Tita's tears *in utero*, induced by the onions, bring on Mama Elena's labor. She suddenly cries out with birth pains and delivers Tita in a freshet of tears that the camera shows from below in close-up flowing off the table, onto the floor and down the stairs. Later the film shows in close-up the grains of salt swept up by the Indian cook Nacha, enough to fill a twenty-kilo sack and serve the needs of the kitchen for months to come. This scene reinforces the links between Tita, tears, salt, and suffering, and between food and emotions.

Soon after Tita's birth, Mama Elena's husband drops dead of a heart attack after a friend suggests that his second daughter was actually fathered by Mama Elena's former lover, "the mulatto." The film cuts to her husband's funeral, where the camera shows Mama Elena sitting on a bench, dressed in black. The camera comes in closer as she opens her blouse and tries to breast-feed her newborn daughter, Tita, with a final close-up shot of her empty breast pulling away from Tita's infant mouth. This is the last time we see Mama Elena engaged in an effort to feed, and it marks the beginning of her despotism in the household where she obviates her need for a man by becoming like one. In one scene she announces that Tita's destiny is to serve her until she dies, and then the camera does a medium shot of Mama Elena's torso, dressed in severe black, her head held high and haughty as she tells Nacha, "Feed the girls; they're hungry." From this point on she never feeds her children and she is shown with food only to command or consume it, typically masculine roles.

Later in the film, just prior to sending the now-married Rosaura and Pedro away to foil Pedro's passion for Tita, there is a close-up shot of a watermelon being smashed open with one forceful blow, exposing the sensual red center. Then the camera shows the Indian servant Chencha walking along with Tita and laughing, saying, "When it comes to breaking things up, your mother is the master." This scene symbolically refers not only to Mama Elena's masculine nature and her breaking up of Pedro and Tita, but also to her own broken extramarital relationship with the mulatto. In another scene, the camera shows Tita and Mama Elena sitting around the table making sausages together when Chencha enters the scene weeping to tell them of the death of Rosaura's and Pedro's infant son Roberto. When Tita starts to cry, Mama Elena states, "I don't want tears," denying the association of emotions with food (and repeating the words she uttered when she ordered Tita to cook Rosaura's wedding feast). When Tita leaps up from the table, crying out in anger against her mother, Mama Elena rises and hits her full force in the face with a spoon. Mama Elena uses food as a path to dominance, not as a form of nurturing or emotional connection.[4]

Mama Elena's assumption of masculine power is represented through rejection of the servile aspects of feeding and cooking, adoption of the patriarchal activities of consumption and control, and her elimination of men. After her husband dies, she dismisses the priest's concerns that she is vulnerable at the ranch without a man by saying, "I've never needed one," and, "It's worse to have chiles without water" than to be without a man. Yet the film opts against female separation from men as a path to liberation by defining Mama Elena's stance as futile and self-defeating. Patriarchal values destroy her—both emotionally and literally. She represses her passion for the mulatto and locks his picture away in a memento box. The denial of love causes her to become ugly and cruel. She sends Rosaura away, severs all connection with Gertrudis, and exiles Tita. Bereft of her three daughters, she dies murdered at the ranch by predatory gringoes who cross the Rio Grande intent on robbery and rape. Mama Elena lives by the sword, and she dies by the sword.

Mama Elena passes on her patriarchal values and power to her first-born daughter Rosaura. When Pedro asks to marry Tita, Mama Elena refuses and offers him Rosaura instead, prompting Chencha to explode, "You can't just exchange tacos for enchiladas!" But Rosaura accepts her mother's will and agrees to marry Pedro, although she knows that he loves Tita. When Mama Elena dies, she leaves Rosaura the ranch, symbol of her wealth and power. Rosaura begins to look uncannily like her mother and continues her repressive and unloving ways.

Rosaura's lack of love is symbolized by her inability to cook, to enjoy food, or to breastfeed her children. Three months after their wedding, Pedro finally agrees to have sex with Rosaura and the next morning she descends to the kitchen announcing that she will cook. She refuses Tita's offer of help, takes her apron, and displaces her. But Rosaura makes an unappealing and distasteful meal that produces disgust and diarrhea in her family members. Her sickening meal juxtaposed to her first act of conjugal union implies that Rosaura lacks love, cannot nurture, and is associated with excrement rather than with love and health. When Tita produces the ambrosial quail in rose petal sauce, Rosaura pronounces, "I feel sick," and leaves the table, symbolically refusing passion and embodying disease. Like her mother, she does not breast feed her children. And she carries on her mother's subjugation of Tita and of emotions because, as the oldest sister, she benefits from inheriting her mother's patriarchal power.

In contrast, the second sister Gertrudis devours Tita's culinary creations, burns with ardor after consuming foods imbued with Tita's amorous longing, and uses these emotions as a springboard to liberation. After consuming the quail in rose-petal sauce, she is so filled with ardor that she ignites the shower room and then runs off with the revolutionary soldier Juan Alejandrez. She lives briefly in a brothel and then joins the revolution and becomes a general. She marries Juan Alejandrez and throughout the film is depicted as his equal, sharing an exuberant appetite for food, sex, and dancing. About her Esquivel says, "Gertrudis represents the first stage of feminism, breaking away, total sexual liberation, in fact a masculinization. She goes out and becomes a part of the revolution. She becomes a general, she participates in the public phase of the revolution, she kills people" (Lowenstein 1994: 594).

Gertrudis loves to eat but does not feed others. She is rarely shown making food, but is often shown eating. When she comes home at Christmas during the revolution she feasts with gusto and says "Revolutions would not be so bad if you could eat at home every day." She cajoles Tita to make her favorite fritters in cream sauce saying, "While I tell you what to do, why don't you fix my fritters." She chooses self-gratification and power over nurturance and thus reverses traditional gender roles. Yet in contrast to Rosaura, she retains allegiance to women and female values by respecting Tita's cooking and encouraging her love for Pedro even though it violates the patriarchal norms of monogamous marriage. She embraces the revolution and its values, including the liberation of women and the legitimization of women's sexuality whether within or outside of marriage.

Tita is the central character in the film, played with a beautiful range of expression by Lumi Cavazos. She lives and speaks through food and exerts potent influence over others through cooking deep emotions into her exquisite dishes. Esquivel says, "Tita makes her own revolution in the family environment ... Tita is completely a transgressor" (Lowenstein 1994: 594, 596). She is constantly able to subvert her mother's dominance with food. For example, when Mama Elena cruelly orders Tita to help Nacha cook

Rosaura's wedding feast, she commands "Not a single tear." But Tita's misery is so great that she cannot help herself from crying and one tear falls into the batter of Pedro and Rosaura's cake. This drop infects the batter with all of Tita's despair. Later in a magnificent wide-angle scene, the assembled wedding guests rush from the table weeping for lost love and then collectively vomit their lifelong regrets into the Rio Grande. Even Mama Elena rushes to her room weeping and there unlocks her secret memento case where she stares lovingly at the photograph of her former lover, the mulatto, Gertrudis's father. All the power of Mama Elena's repression cannot stop Tita's strong feelings from infecting her food and those who consume it.

In another memorable scene the four women are sewing and Rosaura is visibly pregnant. Pedro comes into the room with a bouquet of roses that he gives not to his wife but to Tita to mark her first anniversary as the ranch cook, ignoring the fact that it is also the anniversary of his marriage to Rosaura. Mama Elena orders Tita to throw the roses away but Nacha, whose death caused Tita to succeed her as cook, appears in a vision and tells Tita to prepare quail in rose petal sauce. After hugging the roses, Tita's chest is covered with red scratches, and her blood stains the roses. When she cooks with them, she infuses the quail in rose petal sauce with all of her love for Pedro. This act recalls not only the ensorceling of food reported by Behar (1989) in eighteenth-century Mexico but also the central act of the Catholic Mass—the transubstantiation of the bread and wine into the body and blood of Christ (Valdés 1995: 81). Tita's emotions transubstantiate the food from a simple comestible into a powerful form of communion. When eaten by Tita's family, it acts as a powerful aphrodisiac and produces passionate ardor in all but Rosaura. Mama Elena, however, denies the passion the dish stirs in her by saying coldly, "It has too much salt." Yet again she rushes from the table to gaze longingly at the secret photo of her former lover, the mulatto. By blaming Tita's creation for having excessive salt, which symbolizes life's sorrow and bitterness, she tries to deny passion and regret, but Tita's power to evoke them is stronger than Mama Elena's ability to repress them.

Throughout the movie, Tita's beauty and fecundity are associated with food. While she is serving Christmas rolls, Pedro's amorous gaze makes her feel "how dough feels when it is plunged into boiling oil." Pedro surprises her while she is gathering eggs in her skirt, hoisted up above her knees. When she sees Pedro, Tita drops her skirt and all the eggs fall on him, implying Tita's association with food and fertility. Another time, Tita is grinding corn at the *metate* and Pedro's eyes fall on her breasts; the narrator says they are immediately transformed by his ardor out of a virginal state. In the next scene, Tita begins miraculously to breast-feed the infant Roberto after his wet-nurse is shot. When Mama Elena sends Roberto, Rosaura, and Pedro away to separate Pedro from Tita, the infant Roberto is robbed of his sustenance at Tita's breast and dies because "everything he ate disagreed with him." This scene implies that Tita's feeding has the power of life and death.

After Roberto dies, Tita goes mad with grief and takes refuge, naked and catatonic, in the ranch's dovecote. John Brown, the American doctor, takes her from the ranch to care for her. Tita can no longer speak. Separated from the kitchen and free of her mother's orders, she loses her means of expression. Without her work of chopping, kneading, stirring, and creating, Tita is mute. Eventually healed by John's patient care and Chencha's oxtail soup, Tita regains her voice. She tells Chencha to tell her mother that she will never come back to the ranch and she decides to marry John, doubly refuting her mother's destiny for her.

But after Mama Elena dies at the hands of the men from across the Rio Grande, Tita returns to the ranch for her funeral, as do Pedro and Rosaura. Distressed by her grief, Rosaura gives birth prematurely to a baby girl whom John delivers safely but with the news that Rosaura will have no more children. Rosaura wants to name the baby after Tita, because, she says, her daughter will carry on the family tradition, like Tita, of never marrying and serving her mother. This proclamation infuriates Tita who refuses to let the child bear her name but suggests Esperanza, or Hope, instead. Rosaura is again unable to breastfeed her child so Tita sustains Esperanza by feeding her teas and broths, just as Nacha fed Tita after Mama Elena could not breastfeed her. Tita's rage at Rosaura's self-serving repression permeates her cooking. Rosaura gets fat, begins to belch and fart uncontrollably, has bad breath, and eventually dies from "severe digestive problems" brought on by Tita's powerful anger infused in her cooking.

While anger, sorrow, and regret emanate from Tita's cooking, the film suggests that women's greatest power comes from filling food with love. In the film this power belongs to Mexican women. The American women are unsuccessful cooks and nurturers, and they are women without loving relationships with men. Sue Ellen is John's housekeeper, chastely taking care of him and his son Alex. When John brings Tita to his home to heal her from her mania, he brings her a distasteful looking plate of white food that the camera films in close-up, demonstrating that Sue Ellen's cooking is awful. Her old-maid housekeeper status is linked to her failure to cook well.

John's American Aunt Mary is depicted as caring more about eating than cooking, and this is linked to her lack of emotional understanding. Prior to Tita's planned and later cancelled wedding to John, she invites Aunt Mary to dinner. Aunt Mary raves that not only is Tita beautiful but she is also a wonderful cook. But this meal occurs while Tita is consumed with guilt about having just made love with Pedro. When John questions her she replies that she does not want to discuss her troubles in front of his aunt. He tells her not to worry for not only is Aunt Mary deaf, but "when she eats, she notices nothing." In fact, Aunt Mary interprets Tita's tears as expressing joy, not the conflict and dismay they really express. Aunt Mary is portrayed as obtusely consumed with eating, not altruistically concerned with feeding as the good Mexican women in the film are.

The Indian servants Nacha and Chencha cook for and serve their middle-class, land-owning Mexican employers with uncomplaining altruism. John Kraniauskas (1993: 43) criticizes "the sentimentalized relations between Tita and the female servants Nacha and Chencha" for contributing to a racist representation of the naturalness of "domestic servitude" for Indians reminiscent of how films like *Gone with the Wind* cast service as the natural lot of African Americans. Yet Kraniauskas fails to recognize that the servants take a clear moral position in supporting Tita against the despotism of Mama Elena and that their solidarity is critical to Tita's survival and ultimate triumph. Nacha nurtures the infant Tita with love, teas, and broths after Mama Elena's milk dries up. Later when Mama Elena refuses Pedro's request to marry Tita and gives him Rosaura instead, Nacha comforts Tita by bringing her food as she lies cold and despairing in bed, saying, "Eat, it will make it hurt less." Nacha teaches Tita to cook and thus gives her the power to communicate through food that succors her and enables her to fight back against her mother. The younger Indian servant, Chencha, cures Tita from her madness by bringing her oxtail soup. The film gives the Indian servants little character development and romanticizes them as repositories of traditional wisdom, but it nonetheless defines them positively as women who nurture and uses them to emphasize the importance of bonds between women (Jaffe 1993: 220).

When the neighbor Paquita exclaims on diverse occasions how good Tita's food is, Tita replies, "the secret is to cook it with lots of love." Esquivel comments, "For me the simple act of cooking is, in fact, an act of love … Out of two things you make one thing; you mix the four elements, and out of the four elements you make one single thing, which, to me, is an act of love. Transmitting your emotions intensifies it all the more" (Lowenstein 1994: 605). To cook with lots of love is a fine message, but it leaves open questions about the role of men in the dialectic of feeding and eating. Examination of the two main male characters—Tita's Mexican lover Pedro, and the American doctor John, who asks her in vain to marry him—makes clear the film's problematic definition of men.

Tita loves Pedro passionately. He is the classic Latin lover—handsome, sensual, and passionate. He is her destiny, for Nacha tells her as a tiny infant that the first man who sees her will fall in love with her. Pedro spots Tita at a family party when she is just a girl, and later when she is just fifteen declares his undying love for her and asks her to return it. When she says she needs to think about it, he says, *"L'amor no se pensa, se siente"*—"love is not thought, it is felt." Pedro seems to represent Esquivel's definition of Mexican masculinity—passionate and sensual. But he is also incompetent.

The best plan he can come up with when Mama Elena refuses his request to marry Tita is to marry Rosaura to be near Tita. The film epitomizes Pedro's incompetence in a scene where he tells Tita how his marriage to Rosaura has been a great sacrifice. Tita deflates the nobility of this act when she replies, "I wish you had just kidnapped me." This solution was beyond Pedro, perhaps because of his lack of imagination and his conventional bourgeois view of the world. Pedro is never shown working (Lawless 1997, 233), and he is totally dominated by Mama Elena (Zapata 1997: 212). He resists making love to Rosaura for three months but he shares her bed, eventually has sex with her, and she gets pregnant. Pedro is oblivious to how all this might hurt Tita, but when she announces her plans to marry John, Pedro throws a fit of jealousy. In the film, Mexican men take their love seriously. Pedro gives Tita powerful passion but little else.

John Brown is a sharp contrast to Pedro. Pedro is dark, sensual, and passionate; John is pale, kind, and bland. He is a competent Anglo doctor who expresses his love for Tita through his healing and nurturing abilities. While Pedro cannot seem to do anything right, John is always capable. When Tita goes mad after hearing about the infant Roberto's death, John takes her to his own home to care for her. He gently talks to her, brushes her hair and tries to feed her. He talks to her as an equal and explains at length Brandt's discovery of phosphorus and his Kickapoo Indian grandmother's theories about the emotions. Later, he delivers the infant Esperanza and heals Pedro's burns. When Tita thinks that she has lost Pedro forever she agrees to marry John because she feels "calm" and "safe" with him. Yet after Pedro sees her kissing John, he comes to her in the night and they make passionate love. Later, Tita confesses tearfully to John what she has done. He is forgiving and says that it does not matter to him. John says that if she loves him he will marry her anyway but if she loves Pedro more then he will be the first to congratulate Pedro. Clearly the film thus defines Anglo men as weak. While Mexican men die from the mere thought that they might be cuckolds, as Tita's father does in the film, Anglos forgive and forget, showing they are understanding but effete. The film reverses the traditional outcome of most American movies where the Anglo gets the girl and the Mexican is abandoned. Tita's choice of Pedro, however, shows that the film dichotomizes care and passion in men and values men for passion, not care.

By having Tita choose Pedro, the film also abandons the ideal of reciprocity between men and women.[5] She gives herself to a man who cannot fully give himself to her, both because he has another wife and because he is incapable of nurture. He never feeds or cares for anyone in the film, not even his own children, but is often fed by Tita who also nurses him after he is badly burned. She, not he, is caring, nurturing, and competent. But she nonetheless chooses Pedro rather than John who feeds, nurtures and heals her and shares his ideas with her as well. Rather than reciprocity of nurture between men and women, Esquivel suggests a kind of separate but equal formula. She says

> I am convinced that cooking to me is an inversion of the couple's sexual role. This nurturing that our essence carries, and that our love carries ... this is how the women can, in fact, penetrate the man, this is how it converts, and the man is the passive one, he receives this and for me it is very intense and very erotic. (Lowenstein 1994:605)[6]

Rather than reciprocal nurturing and reciprocal sex, she exalts male and female difference and inter-penetration. While this works in the film for Tita and Pedro, in real life often both cooking and sexual penetration are carried out without mutual affirmation. Women too often cook because they have to, and love dries up under the drudgery. Sharing cooking with men would help liberate it from coercion and make it mutually sustaining.

The film suggests diverse ways that women can gain empowerment through food. It celebrates "reclaiming of the kitchen as a space of creative power rather than merely confinement" (Jaffe 1993: 220) and speaks to, through and about women. Rather than accepting a patriarchal vision that defines the work of women as only mindless drudgery, the film redefines that work as creative, inspiring, and life giving. Her great-niece says at the end of the film, "Tita will continue to live as long as someone cooks her recipes." The film celebrates mutually supportive relationships between women by showing how sharing and passing on recipes can be a subversive source of power.[7] It legitimates women's kitchen work by transforming it into literature in the form of Tita's cookbook and celebrating it as a powerful expression of women's voices. It condemns women who use food only to dominate others by killing off both Mama Elena and Rosaura. By depicting Gertrudis positively the film acknowledges that women's equality with men can come from abandoning the kitchen but rather than promoting that abandonment the film advocates that women gain power through the traditional female role as altruistic and loving nurturers. But in defining male caretaking and feeding as unattractive and unmanly, the film fails to mandate the reciprocity of nurture essential to balanced gender relations. The film is right that the secret is cooking with lots of love but a more progressive message would be to suggest that men and women should mutually feed each other love in diverse and multiple ways.

Appendix

Like Water for Chocolate (Como agua para chocolate) (Mexico 1991). *Director and Producer*: Alfonso Arau. *Screenplay*: Laura Esquivel (based on her novel). *Directors of photography*: Emmanuel Lubezki and Steve Bernstein. *Editors*: Carlos Bolado and Francisco Chiu. *Music*: Leo Brower

Cast

Tita, youngest daughter	Lumi Cavazos
Pedro, Tita's lover	Marco Leonardi
Mama Elena, the mother	Regina Torne
Rosaura, oldest daughter	Yareli Arizmendi
Gertrudis, middle daughter	Claudette Maille
John, the doctor	Mario Ivan Martinez
Nacha, the Indian cook	Ada Carrasco
Chencha, the Indian servant	Pilar Aranda
Esperanza, Rosaura and Pedro's daughter	Sandra Arau
Alex, John's son	Andres Garcia Jr.
Sergeant Treviño	Joaquin Garrido
Juan Alejandrez	Rodolfo Arias
Paquita Lobo	Margarita Isabel
Tita's great neice, the narrator	Arcelia Ramirez
Aunt Mary, John's aunt	Brigida Alexander

Film data are summarized from Kraniauskas (1993).

Notes

1 This is a revised version of Counihan (2001): Tränen, Zorn und Leidenschaft aufkochen; Die Macht von Frauen in dem mexikanishchen Film *Como agua para chocolate—Bittersüsse Schokolade*. M. Kaller-Dietrich and A. Schweighofer-Brauer (eds) *Frauen Kochen: Kulturhistorisch-anthropoologische Blicke auf Köchin, Küche und Essen*, pp. 155–175. Innsbruck: Studienverlag.

2 The book and film are a parody of a mid-nineteenth century Mexican genre of "women's fiction published in monthly installments together with recipes, home remedies ... short poems, moral exhortations ... and the calendar of church observances ... These publications ... are documents that conserve and transmit a Mexican female culture in which the social context and cultural space are particularly for women by women" (Valdés 1995: 78). Through parody, the film transforms this genre to challenge rather than uphold the status quo (Zapata 1997). See also Romney (1993) and Zamudío-Taylor and Guiu (1994).

3 Beoku-Betts (1995) argues that women's food traditions among the Gullah of the Georgia Sea Islands are critical to their cultural identity and endurance. Dash's film *Daughters of the Dust* (1991) also centers on the Gullah. A family reunion picnic calls into question the meaning of tradition as several family members are about to leave the islands for the north.

4 Esquivel says that Elena is "equal to the masculine world and masculine repression, not feminine ... She is also a victim of repression but with all her strength she was unable to rebel against tradition" (Lowenstein 1994: 594).

5 I disagree on this point with Bilbija (1996: 161) who claims that *Like Water for Chocolate* "dismantle[s] that same duality that puts masculinity on one side and femininity on the other ... emphasizing the importance of nurturing for both men and women." She cites only the incident where Gertrudis calls Sergeant Treviño to finish her cream fritters when

Tita goes off to talk to Pedro and does not provide any evidence of Pedro nurturing or cooking.

6   Ruth Behar (1989: 180) also makes the point that using food magic can be a way for women to enter men when she suggests that "women's serving of ensorceled food to men was another kind of reversal, sexual rather than social: a way for women to penetrate men's bodies."

7   Janice Jaffe (1993) cites Susan Leonardi's (1989) reminder that the Latin root of "recipe" is *recipere*, which implies both to give and to receive. Ksenija Bilbija makes this same point when she says, "Isn't the whole idea of the cook book recipe based on sharing?" (1996: 153).

References

BEHAR, R. 1989. Sexual Witchcraft, Colonialism, and Women's Powers: Views from the Mexican Inquisition. A. Lavrin (ed.) *Sexuality and Marriage in Colonial Latin America*, pp. 178–206. Lincoln, NE: University of Nebraska Press.

BEOKU-BETTS, J. A. 1995. We Got Our Way of Cooking Things: Women, Food and the Preservation of Cultural Identity among the Gullah. *Gender and Society* 9: 535–555.

BILBIJA, K. 1996. Spanish American Women Writers: Simmering Identity over a Low Fire. *Studies in Twentieth-Century Literature* 20, (1): 147–165.

COUNIHAN, C. 1999. *The Anthropology of Food and Body: Gender, Meaning and Power*. New York: Routledge.

COUNIHAN, C. 2001. Tränen, Zorn und Leidenschaft aufkochen; Die Macht von Frauen in dem mexikanishchen Film "*Como agua para chocolate*" – "*Bittersüsse Schokolade*." M. Kaller-Dietrich and A. Schweighofer-Brauer (eds) *Frauen Kochen: Kulturhistorisch-anthropoologische Blicke auf Köchin, Küche und Essen*, pp. 155–175. Innsbruck: Studienverlag.

COUNIHAN, C. 2003. Food Contagion. *Slow: the Magazine of the International Slow Food Movement*, 39: 22–25.

COUNIHAN, C. 2004. *Around the Tuscan Table: Food, Family and Gender in Twentieth Century Florence*. New York: Routledge.

DASH, J. 1991. *Daughters of the Dust* (film). American Playhouse, Geechee Girls, and WMG films.

DEVAULT, M. L. 1991. *Feeding the Family: The Social Organization of Caring as Gendered Work*. Chicago, IL: University of Chicago Press.

ELLIS, R. 1983. The Way to a Man's Heart: Food in the Violent Home. A. Murcott (ed.) *The Sociology of Food and Eating*, pp. 164–171. Aldershot: Gower Publishing.

ESQUIVEL, L. 1989. *Como Agua para Chocolate: Novela de entregas mensuales con recetas, amores, y remedios caseros*. Mexico City: Planeta. (Translated by Carol Christensen and Thomas Christensen, *Like Water for Chocolate: A Novel in Monthly Installments, with Recipes, Romances, and Home Remedies*. New York: Doubleday, 1992.)

FRIEDLANDER, J. 1978. Aesthetics of Oppression: Traditional Arts of Women in Mexico. *Heresies* 1(4): 3–9.

JAFFE, J. 1993. Hispanic American Women Writers' Novel Recipes and Laura Esquivel's *Como Agua para Chocolate* (*Like Water for Chocolate*). *Women's Studies* 22(2) 217–231.

KRANIAUSKAS, J. 1993. *Como agua para chocolate* (*Like Water for Chocolate*). *Sight and Sound* 3(10): 42–43.

LAWLESS, C. 1997. Cooking, Community, Culture: A Reading of *Like Water for Chocolate*. A. L. Bower (ed.) *Recipes for Reading: Community Cookbooks, Stories, Histories*, pp. 216–235. Amherst, MA: University of Massachusetts Press.

LEONARDI, S. J. 1989. Recipes for Reading: Summer Pasta, Lobster à la Riseholme, and Key Lime Pie. *Publications of the Modern Language Association of America* 104: 340–347.

LOWENSTEIN, C. 1994. Revolución interior al exterior: An Interview with Laura Esquivel. *Southwest Review* 79(4): 592–607.

ROMNEY, J. 1993. Eating Her Gut Out. *New Statesman and Society*, (6)272: 33–34.

VALDÉS, M. E. DE. 1995. Verbal and Visual Representation of Women: *Como agua para Chocolate/Like Water for Chocolate*. *World Literature Today* 69(1): 78–82.

WITT, D. 1999. *Black Hunger: Food and the Politics of US Identity*. New York: Oxford University Press.

ZAMUDÍO-TAYLOR, V. and GUIU, I. 1994. Criss-Crossing Texts: Reading Images in *Like Water for Chocolate*. C. A. Noriega and S. Ricci (eds) *The Mexican Cinema Project*. Los Angeles, CA: UCLA Film and Television Archive.

ZAPATA, M. 1997. *Like Water for Chocolate* and the Free Circulation of Clichés. R. A. Young (ed.) *Latin American Postmodernisms*, pp. 205–220. Amsterdam: Rodopi.

Helene **Brembeck**

Göteborg University

··Home to McDonald's

Upholding the Family Dinner with the Help of McDonald's

Fast food is regularly referred to as a symbol of the decline of cooking skills, families and the community at the dinner table. With inspiration from theories on domestication and Actor Networks, and using examples from studies from McDonald's in Sweden, this paper argues that a McDonald's restaurant can in fact be regarded as a home and the meals eaten there as "proper" family meals. A meal at the restaurant is for many parents the easiest way of upholding family life, but also of creating "family" and "home" in new ways.

Introduction and Points of Departure

There seems to be a lot of reasons why McDonald's could not be "home" and why a meal at McDonald's could not be equated with a family meal. Swedish ethnologist Anna Burstedt points to the simple fact that consumers want to experience something different when they choose going out to eat, as opposed to the everyday meal eaten in the kitchen at home. In the restaurant one should be able to sit down without having to worry about dishes, preparation and screaming children (Burstedt, 2004). Besides, the food at McDonald's is not home made but industrially processed and thus generally regarded as more complicated, non-natural and artificial (Fredriksson, 2000), and it is also branded. So dinner at McDonald's is pure leisuretime consumption, whereas dinner at home is much more connected to production. Not just the production of food, but of "the family," in terms of etiquette, manners, values and gender and generation, and also in terms of emotional bonds created by the community of eating together and by the food stuff as objectifying love (Murcott, 1983; DeVault, 1991; Miller, 1998). That food is such an important medium for communicating moral and ethical values, not least to children, and that cooking is often regarded as an act of love, especially from mother to children, are important reasons why fast food is referred to regularly as a symbol of decline—of cooking skills, families, and the community at the dinner table (Bell and Valentine, 1997; Jönsson, 2004). From this point of view it seems certain that places like McDonald's restaurants could never be regarded as home, and the meals eaten there could not be regarded as "proper" family meals.

Doing ethnographic fieldwork at McDonald's restaurants in Sweden, however, has led me to another conclusion. As places invested with meaning, value, joy, and sociality McDonald's restaurants are genuine and authentic local rooms, maybe even "homes", for many families (cf. Caldwell. 2004). Moreover, the routines and the materiality of the restaurant offer ways of upholding family life but also of creating everyday, family life, and home in new ways that are in accordance with the demands and rhythms of today's world. My argument is thus that McDonald's restaurants can in fact be regarded as home and the meals eaten there as "proper" family meals for some families.

In my own discipline, ethnology, a North and Central European little sister to anthropology, the 1990s brought the "linguistic turn," characterizing many disciplines in the humanities and the social sciences at this time. Culture, understood as an underlying grammar, was something to be read out of texts, objects, everyday conversations, and so forth sometimes resulting in more of an armchair ethnology than the traditional fieldwork. Methods like cultural analysis, set forth by professors Orvar Löfgren, Jonas Frykman and Billy Ehn in books like *Culture Builders* (Frykman and Löfgren, 1987), *On Holiday* (Löfgren, 1999) and *Magic, Culture and the New Economy* (Löfgren and Willim, 2005), gave, and still give, Swedish ethnology an international reputation. Discourse analysis, following Michel Foucault, and, concerning gender, Judith Butler, also holds a high reputation among Swedish ethnologists.

In recent years, however, there has been somewhat of a turning back to materiality and ethnography. One inspiration is material culture studies as advocated by for example British anthropologists Daniel Miller and Alison Clarke in books like *Tupperware* (Clarke, 1999) and *Home Possessions* (Miller, 2001), and journals like *Journal of Material Culture* and *Home Cultures*. A more recent inspiration is European versions of Science and Technology Studies (STS) like the French Actor-Network Theory (ANT) of Bruno Latour and Michel Callon, and the British counterpart sociology of translation, with John Law as a prominent predecessor. The accusation of too much armchair ethnology has led to a rising interest in ethnographic fieldwork inspired by George Marcus's multi-sited fieldwork approach (Marcus, 1995). This also reflects my own path as a researcher for almost fifteen years, focusing on matters of family, childhood and parenthood in an increasingly commercialized Swedish context; I started by doing cultural analysis, I wrote my thesis on discourses, and I am now increasingly interested in matters of materiality, and especially in ANT, and in doing multi-sited field work.

Studying McDonald's in Sweden

This interest has been guiding the topic of my study for the past three years: parents and children dining at McDonald's. The restaurant seemed to me to be the perfect place to be—a place where I could have a Coke or a cup of coffee while watching people coming and going, having dinners and conversations, celebrating birthday parties, and so on. The restaurant can also be regarded as a node in an almost worldwide network involving not only restaurants, customers and staff, but also for example food, package, transports, commercials and technology, a perfect place for doing multi-sited fieldwork and pondering the agency of not only humans but also, for instance, foodstuff and technologies. In this article I will, however, primarily stick to one particular restaurant, a drive-in situated in Göteborg, the second largest city in Sweden with about 500,000 inhabitants. In Sweden McDonald's is not connected with poverty; rather it is a place where people from all social classes go once in a while, especially teenagers and parents with small children (Brembeck, 2003). In particular the McDrives in suburbia have a middle-class clientele. Poor people tend not to have cars and to live in rented apartments in the city outskirts, and thus rather go to instore McDonald's in shopping malls. In fact, people like young single mothers might not go there at all, or maybe just to have a cup of coffee and to treat the children to a rare Happy Meal. McDonald's is too expensive if you are on a tight budget.

My study of McDonald's is part of a larger research program called Commercial Cultures in an Ethnological and Economical Perspective, carried out at the Center for Consumer Science at Göteborg University (www.cfk.gu.se). As part of my project I have assembled a lot of information gained by observing restaurants, interviewing executives, staff, and customers, studying the homepage, and collecting promotional objects. During the spring of 2003 I had the opportunity of taking part in several children's birthday parities at one particular restaurant. I was video filming and taking photographs just like the rest of the adults/parents. I also took field notes using a diary and had lots of small talk with the parents while they were waiting to bring their children home. I had met some of these parents on several occasions at the restaurant and I now decided to ask them to help me with my research by documenting an "ordinary visit" to the restaurant with their children, using disposable cameras. Ten families agreed to partake and after having exposed the films, I decided to meet with each of the families on their next visit to the restaurant to watch and discuss the snapshots. I equipped myself with a tape recorder and some questions in case the conversation would run short. The ethnography in this article is mainly from this co-researching endeavor, but the concluding arguments are of course also based on the large amount of further data and impressions gathered during my fieldwork. But let's first give voice to the Haglind family (the name is of course fictional), whom I met at the restaurant on a beautiful summer's eve in August of 2004.

A Part of Everyday Life

::

"How does it actually happen when you decide to go to McDonald's?" The Haglinds, mother, father, son and daughter, turn silent and look confused. We have decided to meet at "their" restaurant, a drive-in close to a large shopping mall outside the city. They usually go there twice a month, which makes them fit the average for Swedish families (Brembeck, 2003). They live, like most of the customers this late summer's eve, in the residential area of terraced houses nearby. They are on their way home, the parents have picked up the son from the handball training session, and the daughter from the after-school recreation center, and now they are sitting relaxed with their dinner at the table; salad for mother, Big Mac for father and son, and a Happy Meal for the six-year-old daughter; "with chicken nuggets, not hamburgers," she states. We are crowding together at a table for four and the son is fetching another chair. I have taken out my tape recorder, and suspended the little microphone on an empty Coca-Cola cup. The clock is close to six, the evening sun is shining through the windows, and inside the restaurant a peaceful mood is spreading despite a fairly high sound level. In a corner the TV set is on. This is one of the very last days of the Olympics in Athens 2005, and two wrestlers dressed in red and a blue garments are grappling together. The restaurant is more than half full. It is mostly families with children, like the Haglinds, who have chosen to have their dinner at McDonald's, and the dinner conversation is going on. I hear a dad at an adjacent table asking his son about his day, and questioning about the new pedagogues at the recreation center. Haglind's neighbors are seated a couple of tables away, and I have to wait for a while on my interview while the two families are coordinating the ride to school for their youngest ones.

I have met with the Haglinds before, and they are a cheerful and talkative bunch, enjoying being the center of my interest. But now all four of them are silent and look at me in confusion. "Is it different?" I ask, trying to help. I see them reflecting and looking at each other. "Maybe it is your children nagging?" I try again turning towards the children. But no, "not usually", eleven-year-old Calle tells me. Helpful as they are to me, as I try to explore the place of McDonald's in the everyday life of Swedish families, they start discussing with each other. "Is it maybe on weekends when everybody is at home? Or when they have done some errands, or on the way home from the handball training session like this time?" They all agree, however, that there are no discussions or conflicts about the visits to McDonald's and that is it not decided in advance before leaving home. It is something that simply happens when you start feeling hungry. This is something they have in common with the rest of the families I have met during my study. A visit to McDonald's is nothing decided on beforehand, nothing you plan for or long for, nothing you negotiate with the family members. It is something that simply happens. Certainly, many parents agree that the children's hunger is the trigger: "It is when the 'hunger crisis' occurs, and it always does after a couple of hours in town, that is when you end up at McDonald's," as Anna, a women I met the night before at the same restaurant expressed it. But Anna also agrees that it is not something you plan in advance.

Investigating the Ordinary
: :

Things that "just happen" are nothing new to me as an ethnologist. On the contrary, the investigation of the ordinary, the obvious, the unproblematic is somewhat of an ethnological speciality, as is showing how matters of course are built step-by-step, over longer periods of time, where ideas and actions are linked to the various prerequisites of everyday life (Frykman and Löfgren, 1996). The families I have met at McDonald's have not equipped themselves for a day in the city with their children by bringing a packed lunch or by fitting the visit in between two meals at home. They don't need to because they know where the restaurants are situated. And if they don't the smallest child of three years of age is already able to recognize the "golden arches" that most certainly will show up along the shopping route of the ordinary family. Besides, there are Burger King, Pizza Hut and lots of other options. There is no need to plan in advance. Inside you know exactly what to expect. You know what it looks like, you know the menu, you know the taste of a Big Mac before taking the first bite, you know exactly how to behave at the counter, and how to balance the order on the tray without overturning anything, you can feel the weight of a large Coke before lifting it to take a drop, you know how to manage the ketchup pump and the napkin stand and you are used to shoving the litter the right way into the recycling bin. There is no need for thinking because you have done it so many times before; it has turned into unproblematic everyday knowledge, the way tying ones shoes or pouring the breakfast cereals has.

Supporting Assemblies of Actants
: :

Habits like slipping into McDonald's are not passive but always involve an active process of creating meaning, as is highlighted in Melissa Caldwell's study of the introduction of McDonald's in Moscow. Ordinary Muscovite consumers have incorporated McDonald's and its products as significant and meaningful elements in their social life, she argues (Caldwell, 2004: 6). From an ANT-perspective (Latour, 1999), the habit can be studied as an assembly or a small network of entities, or more precisely, an order of relations of certain entities or "actants," a series, an ordered space or territory, a rhythm or a pulse that is repeated in certain ways creating a tune that is easy to follow (Brown and Capdevila, 1999). Since actants might be human as well as non-human, ideas as well as technologies, the rhythm of ordered relations at the drive-in restaurant include, among other things the car, the restaurant, the hamburgers, the staff training courses, the child-friendly furnishing, the biological and cultural processes of hunger, discourses on children, parenthood and family, the capability of the fluorescent lamp to bend in the shape of a "M," the capability of the child to memorize visual symbols, the supermarket, the full-time work of the parents, consumer society, the cupboards requesting to be filled, the work-free Saturday, the long road to the nearest grocery store, the tiredness of the parents. Many different actants are coworking to generate the easiness with which the parents slip into the restaurant.

The feeling of meaning is generated when everything fits, when the habit and the special assemblage it involves solves problems, makes everyday life easier, renders confirmation, happiness and satisfaction. Even if the parents I have met have had a hard time recapitulating the process leading up to the visit to the restaurant, there is total agreement about the values the visit holds: it is easy, convenient, fast, and quite inexpensive for a large family. Moreover you always know what to expect, the children know what to expect, no unpleasant surprises are waiting inside. And there is something for everybody. The parents know that the children like the food, eat it and are satisfied. This is especially important for parents, where the evening meal at home often is turned into a daily fight. Besides, the food is considered tasty. The adults often go there for lunches or buy meals for themselves from the drive-in, because they think McDonald's food tastes nice, not every day of the week, but now and then.

For families with toddlers the bibs and the microwave ovens are effective actants. Shopping with a one-year-old and a three-year-old child is an extensive project lasting for several hours, and many parents argue that these trips would be much more difficult to carry through without McDonald's. Simply finding another restaurant where kids are as welcome and smoking is not allowed is difficult. At McDonald's you never have to worry if your child is noisy and makes a mess at the table. There are really no good alternatives to McDonald's, they argue.

Making Life Easier

The rest of the day is also influenced in a positive way by having a meal at McDonald's, not least for the women who were the ones doing most of the housework in the families I interviewed. "It is really quite nice when you get home after having done a lot of errands that you have already eaten so that you don't have to start by making dinner," one woman told me. Her eleven-year-old son agrees, and argues that it is a great difference if you get home and have already eaten at McDonald's because then you have more time and can start with your hobbies right away instead of having to wait for the dinner. To be spared the dreary intervening time, the waiting, the preparing, cooking, table laying and the stress of having hungry and whining family members wandering around means a lot. Having a meal at McDonald's means a quicker way of reaching the goal of the family gathered around the dinner table eating in peace (hopefully). This might be considered a way of promoting "instant gratification" (Bauman, 2002), that the morality of postponing pleasures, work before fun, of former days (Brembeck, 1992) is giving way to hedonistic pleasures. But it is also possible to interpret it as a way to organize a life with many offers and a constant lack of time. To be spared the dreary intervening time can be a rational way of handling a life of time pressure. It can also be a way of generating time for relaxation and interests of your own beside work or school and can thus enable you to be better prepared to endure another day's work. To answer the "hunger cries" of the children with a visit to McDonald's was also for many parents, especially mothers, a way of expressing good motherhood. Parents wanted to give their children something they enjoyed, to please them in today's world, which is considered stressful not only for the parents themselves but also for their children. The visit to the restaurant was also partly seen as a compensation for the tough day at school or at the daycare institution, the long working days of the parents and their tiredness at home.

Just Like at Home

Few myths are harder to disturb than that of the happy nuclear family: mother, father, and two rosy-cheeked children, gathered in the soft lamplight around the dinner table, intimately sharing both food, and the events of the day, and its hidden aspects such as the upholding of the gender and generational order, where adults, especially fathers, knows best and mother is the expert on relations. For many families the McDonald's meal was the easiest way to achieve this ideal in its entirety. Few parents and children agreed that having a meal at McDonald's was different from eating at home. The behavior at the table was the same, as were the topics of conversation, and the time spent on eating. Most family members had not in fact reflected on the possibility that there should be such a difference, arguing that McDonald's was just like being at home. This is also in accordance with my own impressions from the restaurants. The atmosphere was generally calm, homely, and familiar. The families often knew each other; they were living in the same neighbourhood, and the children were friends from school or day care and the mood ranged from that of the friendly local restaurant with fairly loud voices and cheeriness to a sober and quiet murmuring. Few parents felt stressed by the high pace, and sound level at the restaurants, most in fact looked bewildered when I put the question, and they argued that the only time a visit at the restaurant was stressful was if there were no free tables available and they had to wait with tired feet, an empty stomach, and dissatisfied children.

It was only in the longer interviews I made, where the parents were given more time for reflections, that some differences between eating at home and at McDonald's appeared. Maybe there was less fuss at the restaurant because there were so many other distractions, so many other things to look at for the children, and also less tiresome discussion about, for example, finishing the food, the parents figured. At McDonald's everybody is sitting calmly at the table eating. There are so many other things to look at, and so many other activities beside making a fuss about the food, sulking, and bickering with your brothers, and sisters. The restaurant is a place for food and relaxation where there is little room for family disputes. The actants of the McDonald's restaurant are contributing to stabilizing everyday life, helping the family to live up to the ideal of the happy family for a moment, the materiality of the restaurant is stabilizing life. Without the chairs and the tables in their fixed positions, the food coming quickly to the table, the other customers, the TV in its corner, the children jumping in the ballroom, or passing by carrying interesting Happy Meal offers, this would have been much more difficult. The McDonald's visit turns into a way to shape the family in consumer society.

Piling Black Boxes

Most children also agree that the parents too are much like at home, neither stricter nor more kind hearted, although there is of course no room for any obvious exercise of power in the public, normative space of the restaurant. But there were in fact a few examples of the opposite, the children using the invisible normative boundaries of how parents should and should not behave, into a power-play with their parents. Carola, one of the mothers I interviewed, was one of the few parents, who did not like to go to McDonald's. She liked the food but felt that the atmosphere was stressful and not very inviting but she still went there at regular intervals because her daughters wanted to. Her own favourite was Burger King. She felt uncomfortable at McDonald's, she told me. She felt stressed and always finished the food in a hurry. This is not what she herself would choose. She liked the food, and often used the McDrive, but considered the atmosphere pressing and not very nice. The children liked it though. Sofia, her eldest daughter, was stressing her mother by very, very slowly picking the fries one by one, and very slowly chewing them while looking untroubled, and relaxed, and now and then taking a quick look at her mother. Maybe that is why she is so uneasy, Carola says. She herself wants the meal to be quickly finished but Sofia delays it. The visit to the restaurant is turned into a hidden power play, where Sofia is all the time stretching the limits of her self-determination, protected by the invisible conventions of not raising your voice too loud and not using any physical means in the public space of the restaurant. For Sofia the pieces of French fries were actants in her attempts at challenging parental authority, and creating a larger space for actions for herself. Family relations are renegotiated; maybe even a process of equalizing is going on, driven by the nice relaxing feeling of being just like everybody else, of living up to the standard of normality for a while.

Another way of looking upon Sofia's behaviour is that she is piling many "black boxes" on her side. A "black box" according to Latour contains agreements on how to understand reality, taken-for-granted ideas, no longer open for questioning, which have been materialized in societal institutions; in ways to behave and to think, in institutions like the school, the family, the media; and physically, in buildings, furniture, clothes and the planning of a restaurant's interior design (Latour, 1998). Sofia's "black boxes" contain ideas of the democratic family with good relations between parents and children; values of not raising your voice too loud in public, the child-friendly environment of the restaurant announcing the fact that here is a family caring for its children. On top of all her black boxes Sofia can rule her mother, and make her hide her indignation, and make her stay at the table until her daughter has finished her fries, even though she is boiling with rage and feels more and more stressed and uneasy inside. No wonder she often chooses the McDrive instead, because she considers this "less stressful." In the context of the home the generational order is easier to uphold. Carola feels split in an awkward way between the wish to be a good parent and give in to the wishes of her children and her need for a more distinct parental authority, to which the children submit.

At the restaurant there were many examples of the performance of traditional gender roles, for example several examples of fathers benignly inquiring about the day at school and the children politely responding, while mothers were occupied with wiping their baby's mouths and keeping the table tidy. But the environment also generates a more equal relation between the spouses. It is most often the mother who supervises the children's food intake but she is relieved of the requirement to cook and to wash the dishes, and may spend time on her own interests when the family gets back home. As the food is eaten with your fingers, this makes for a more equal relation between parents, and children; everybody is eating on equal terms, and even really small children not only "want" but "can do." The democratic potential of eating with your fingers undermines the generational order (Wenzer, 2004). It is thus quite possible to argue that a visit to McDonald's is a part of everyday life but also a way of changing it in different ways; that the restaurant is a way of upholding family life, but also of creating "family" and "home" in new ways; that the visit to the restaurant is a way to create an everyday life in accordance with the demands and rhythm of today's world.

References

BAUMAN, Z. 2002. *Society under Siege.* London: Polity Press.
BELL, D. and VALENTINE, G. 1997. *Consuming Geographies. We Are Where We Eat.* London: Routledge.
BREMBECK, H. 1992. *Efter Spock. Uppfostringsmönster idag (After Spock. Patterns of Upbringing Today).* Göteborg: Etnologiska föreningen Västsverige.
BREMBECK, H. 2003. I Skuggan av "M". Berättelser om McDonald's (In the Shadow of "M". Tales about McDonald's). *Kulturella Perspektiv* 1: 5–13.
BROWN, S. D. and CAPDEVILA, R. 1999. Perpetuum mobile. Substance, Force and the Sociology of Translation. In J. Law and J. Hassard (eds) *Actor Network Theory and After.* Oxford: Blackwell.
BURSTEDT, A. 2001. Platsen är serverad! K. Hansen and K. Salomonsson (eds) *Fönster mot Europa. Platser och identiteter.* Lund: Studentlitteratur.
BURSTEDT, A. 2004. What 'Time' do we Eat? Some Examples of the Relationship between Time and Food. P. Lysaght (ed.) *Changing Tastes. Food in Culture and the Process of Industrialization.* Basel: Verlag der Schweizerischen Gesellschaft für Volkskunde.
CALDWELL, M. L. 2004. Domesticating the French Fry: McDonald's and consumerism in Moscow. *Journal of Consumer Culture* 4(1): 5–26.
CLARKE, A. J. 1999. *Tupperware. The Promise of Plastic in 1950s America.* Washington, DC: Smithsonian Institute Press.
DEVAULT, M. 1991. *Feeding the Family. The Social Organisation of Caring as Gendered Work.* Chicago, IL: University of Chicago Press.
FREDRIKSSON, C. 2000. Den designade potatisen. Kulturella perspektiv på genmodifierade kulturväxter. S. Lundin and L. Åkesson (eds) *Arvets kultur.* Lund: Nordic Academic Press.
FRYKMAN, J. and LÖFGREN, O. 1987. *Culture Builders. A Historical Anthropology of Middle-Class Life.* New Brunswick, NJ: Rutgers University Press.
FRYKMAN, J. and LÖFGREN, O. 1996. *Force of Habit. Explaining Everyday Culture.* Bromley: Chatwell-Bratt.
JÖNSSON, H. 2004. Food in "Experience Economy". P. Lysaght (ed.) *Changing Tastes. Food in Culture and the Process of Industrialization.* Basel: Verlag der Schweizerischen Gesellschaft für Volkskunde.
LATOUR, B. 1998. *Artefaktens återkomst.* Stockholm: Nerenius & Santérus.
LATOUR, B. 1999. On recalling ANT. Complexity, Naming and Topology J. Law and J. Hassard (1999), *Actor Network Theory and After.* Oxford: Blackwell.
LÖFGREN, O. 1990. Huvudentréer och köksingångar I kulturstudiet N.O. Finneman and H. Horstböll (eds) *Delkulturer.* Århus: Århus Universitetsforlag.
LÖFGREN, O. 1999. *On Holiday. A History of Vacationing.* Berkeley, CA: University of California Press.
LÖFGREN, O and WILLIM, R. 2005. *Magic, Culture and the New Economy.* Oxford: Berg.
MARCUS, G. 1995. Ethnography in/of the World System. The emergence of Multi-sited Ethnography. *Annual Reviews of Anthropology* 24: 95–117.
MILLER, D. 1998. *A Theory of Shopping.* London: Polity Press.
MILLER, D. 2001. *Home Possessions. Material Culture Behind Closed Doors.* Oxford: Berg.
MURCOTT, A. (ed.). 1983. *The Sociology of Food and Eating.* Aldershot: Gower.
OHNUKI-TIERNEY, E. 1997. McDonald's in Japan: Changing Manners and Etiquette. J. L. Watson (ed) *Golden Arches East. McDonald's in East Asia.* Stanford, CA: Stanford University Press.
WATSON, J. L. (ed.) 1997. *Golden Arches East. McDonald's in East Asia.* Stanford, CA: Stanford University Press.

WENZER, J. 2004. The Deterritorialization of the Being Child. H. Brembeck, B. Johansson and J. Kampmann (eds) *Beyond the Competent Child. Exploring Contemporary Childhoods in the Nordic Welfare Societies.* Roskilde: Roskilde University Press.

Commentary

Kelly **Donati**
Globalism Institute
RMIT University

The Pleasure of Diversity in Slow Food's Ethics of Taste

The aim of this paper is to open up the debate about Slow Food's ethics of taste by considering the way in which the Slow Food subject relates to its cultural "other." Drawing on four recent articles on Slow Food in *Food, Culture and Society* as well as examples of Slow Food's activities at the local and international level, I wish to demonstrate how Slow Food's efforts to develop an ethics of taste are, to some extent, undermined by its failure to adequately challenge its own elitism and privilege. I argue that the challenge for Slow Food is to recognize its own heritage of privilege derived from an economic system shaped by imperialism and to actively resist nostalgic renderings of the "other," however well intentioned, which run the risk of fetishizing cultural diversity and sentimentalizing struggles for cultural or economic survival. This requires more meaningful dialogue between Slow Food and those it seeks to support in order to create a space of mutual respect and recognition of difference.

The Slow Food Agenda

At a Slow Food festival held in Victoria, Australia in July 2003, Slow Food Governor of Australia James Broadway spoke at a forum on sustainable food production, describing Slow Food as a guerrilla organization that was antagonistic to the speed-obsessed nature of global capitalism or the "universal folly of the Fast Life."[1] With its efficient production lines and synthetic uniformity of flavors, fast food embodies for Slow Food a disregard in advanced capitalist economies for the earth's natural rhythms and an indifference to the slow pleasures of everyday life.[2] Slow Food's agenda is not to rid the world of fast food or to undo the globalization of today's food systems—an impossible task, in any case—but rather to change the rules of the game so that taste, cultural identity and regional individuality are not assimilated into, and homogenized by, a global food culture devoid of diversity and pleasure. Slow Food's philosophy is underpinned by an understanding of pleasure as a right rather than a privilege and which places cultural and ecological diversity at the center of its ethics of taste. Since taking on the issue of cultural and biological diversity, Slow Food founder Carlo Petrini believes that Slow Food's journey has come "full circle: the new epicures have become ecological gastronomes," transforming the gastronomic connoisseur into an ethical and political agent.[3]

The four papers on Slow Food in the Fall 2004 issue of *Food, Culture and Society* (vol. 7, issue 2) examine whether Slow Food is positioned to achieve its objectives and whether the organization can challenge, or offer any real resistance to, the inequities of the global food supply today. Julie Labelle, Rachel Laudan, Janet Chrzan and Marie Sarita Gaytán differ in the extent to which they believe Slow Food can engender change in the global food system, expressing a range of positions from deep skepticism to cautious optimism. However, they share similar concerns about the elite nature of Slow Food's membership, its nostalgic approach to protecting tradition and a limited engagement with the broader issues of food politics, particularly Slow Food USA from which Chrzan and Gaytán draw on many of their personal experiences and observations.

My aim in this commentary is to open up the debate about Slow Food's ethics of taste by considering its relationship with and representations of the developing world. With Slow Food's membership comprised predominantly of upper-middle-class members, I question the extent to which Slow Food is truly subverting the industrialized food supply and suggest that there is a tendency to fetishize cultural diversity in order to satisfy the appetites of a privileged minority. I analyze Slow Food's representations of nominees for the Award for Biodiversity to reveal traces of a paradoxical phenomenon described by ethnographer Renato Rosaldo as "nostalgia ... often found under imperialism, where people mourn the passing of what they themselves have transformed."[4] I also turn to bell hooks who expresses wariness towards the pleasure that cultural diversity offers Western culture. Returning to Labelle, Laudan, Chrzan and Gaytán, I then examine the relationship between Slow Food USA and its own exoticized, cultural "other," the European working class, which is constructed as more authentic and culturally richer than its American counterparts. By drawing on examples from the organization's activities at the local and international level I hope to demonstrate how Slow Food's efforts to develop an ethics of taste are, to some extent, undermined by its failure to challenge adequately its own elitism and privilege.

Imperial Nostalgia

: :

Slow Food has not been without its critics, who argue that its agenda to protect culinary traditions is misguided and, in some cases, misinformed. Jones *et al.* suggest that Slow Food's use of tradition "romantically harks back to illusory images of a rural idyll or utopian past in which people and nature lived together in simple harmony."[5] This is a criticism similarly expressed by Laudan who has accused Slow Food of "culinary luddism" that relies upon an idealized, nostalgic view of the past and a distorted version of history.[6] Nostalgia, however, is not always such a bad thing. For cultures under threat or undergoing rapid change, the act of looking into the past is important for forging new cultural or national pathways and avoiding a repetition of past mistakes or injustices. Nostalgia is not limited to looking back to a better time but is part of imagining the future. Rather than representing a naïve celebration of invented traditions, Slow Food's use of tradition constitutes for Alison Leitch "socially productive excavations of the past," which are important to ensuring that debate around the cultural politics of food in Europe remains on the table in the future.[7] Rob Wilson and Wimal Dissanayake similarly see nostalgia as "a critical tool" for resisting the homogenizing forces of globalization, so long as "one is cognizant of the newer forces of domination and wary of sentimental idealizations."[8] Nostalgia becomes problematic when it is not accompanied by a critical awareness of how easily the imperialist politics of the past are repeated and perpetrated on others, even in genuine attempts to forge more ethical cultural and economic relationships.

Rosaldo challenges the neutrality of nostalgia, arguing that "innocent" mourning for the loss of traditional cultures is a Western phenomenon that functions to "transform the colonial agent into an innocent bystander."[9] Arif Dirlik argues that global capitalism remains deeply imbued with the values of European culture and its imperial past and has emerged as a form of new imperialism that works to "admit different cultures into the realm of capital only to break them down and to remake them in accordance with" the cultural, political and economic needs of the dominant culture.[10] Throughout the history of imperialism, food has been a powerful cultural and economic force that is, according to Elspeth Probyn, deeply "imbricated in nation-building" and pivotal to "the production of geo-political inequities."[11] Petrini is the first to recognize the role of imperialism in creating the inequities of the global food system today:

> [H]ow complex are the economic and social issues in countries where two waves of colonization have had a devastating effect on agricultural practices and food ... the greatest harm was done during the second wave of colonization, with the imposition of food diets and customers which were totally alien to the territory.[12]

Addressing these global issues requires political activism as well as change at a personal level; it involves, as Petrini describes, "learning to choose differently, even to live differently ... embracing variety and diversity."[13] But what are the implications of placing diversity at the centre of an ethics of taste?

Eating the Other

In *Black Looks: Race and Representation,* hooks offers a critical analysis of the consumption of difference in white American culture, specifically the desire for, and pleasure of, contact with African-American culture and other forms of cultural otherness. hooks' analysis of racial relations in North America is relevant to other relations of cultural difference, particularly where this difference is marked by historical disparities in power created by colonialism. Like Rosaldo whose work she draws upon, hooks is deeply suspicious of the Western yearning for cultural diversity. The pleasure of contact with the "other" works to counteract the homogeneity of Western culture and allays the "guilt of the past, even takes the form of a defiant gesture where one denies accountability and historical connection" with injustices of the past.[14] hooks cites as an example the use of ethnicity in the successful Benetton ads of the 1990s, a campaign that targeted a predominantly white, upper-middle class demographic. Benetton clothing offered "the seduction of difference," providing the white consumer a satisfying sense of political progressiveness without the risk of having to "relinquish forever one's mainstream positionality."[15] In other words, cultural otherness is transformed into a source of fetishized pleasure without critically examining or challenging the complicity of Western culture in the racial marginalization or cultural appropriation of difference.

The tendency in Western culture to romanticize the cultural "other" as spiritually or culturally richer is deeply problematic for hooks who writes that "the Other is coded as having the capacity to be more alive, as holding the secret that will allow those who venture and dare to break with the cultural *adhedonia*"—that is, the incapacity for pleasure or happiness—to experience true "sensual and spiritual renewal."[16] The fear of cultural *adhedonia* is at the heart of the Slow Food ethos:

> In a world dominated by hegemonic forces ... our agricultural and food heritage becomes a significant asset, and we have to actively defend its authenticity and favor the development of the territories in which it is rooted. To ... grasp its manifold connections with the nature of human settlements and their artistic treasures, to savor its products without turning them into cult objects, is the only way to build a relationship with its guardians and rediscover serene conviviality.[17]

The threat to the pleasure of diversity is a function of a culture of accumulation and consumption that grows anxious about the homogeneity engendered by its own capitalist economy, yet to pursue the "serene conviviality," as Slow Food suggests, through relationships with the guardians of diversity, fails to subvert the "mainstream positionality" of its members.[18] For hooks, this understanding of the pleasure of diversity is the equivalent of using cultural difference to spice up the "dull dish that is mainstream white culture."[19]

Representations of the "Other"

The tendency to romanticize cultural difference leads to problematic representations of the "other" in Slow Food's international publications. *Slow Ark* and *PremioSlowFood,* the reporting mechanisms for Presidia projects, recount inspiring stories of men and women dedicated to preserving disappearing food traditions and protecting the earth's food diversity. These are narratives of hope in which nominees are often described as having exceptional qualities or unique characteristics. In the foreword of *PremioSlowFood*, Petrini describes the Slow Food Award nominees as:

> ... men and women who have cultivated a dream with uncommon energy and dedication. We have tracked them down and noticed the enthusiasm that shines in their eyes and gives an edge to their voices, the eloquence of their hands ... After meeting us and hearing about the award, they invariably insisted that our visit alone was gratification enough for them.[20]

Though intending to be respectful, even reverential, the description of these special qualities merely stands for their otherness, and the assumption of their gratitude reveals a deeply paternalistic approach to the very people whom Slow Food seeks to support.

This is not an isolated example. In *Slow Ark*, Scaffidi describes an uneasy experience during an interview in Argentina in which the interviewee turns to Scaffidi after describing his life story and asks, "¿Y vos?" Clearly disarmed, Scaffidi responds:

> My first reaction was to pull down the shutters ... ("I'm asking the questions"), but I could sense that I had to answer. I did answer, summing up my existence in three minutes flat. It sounded more like a badly drafted resume than a chat between two friends ... It was all over in a few minutes, and I am sure my interviewee thought no more about the episode. But I still remember how uneasy I felt.[21]

A simple question provokes an entire article. Unable to offer a meaningful response to her Argentinian friend, Scaffidi goes on to take her hat off to the people who answer her endless questions, patiently enduring the "minor, if well-received, violence that we perpetuate on the individuals we are interviewing."[22] Despite her awareness of the metaphorical violence of the interview, Scaffidi feels uneasy relinquishing her position of authority as the interviewer. Attempting to resolve her uneasiness, Scaffidi expresses her admiration for the hard work they do: "not only are they doing a crucially important, and often very difficult, job" but they also "go to work in places only a fool would settle to live, if there was any choice."[23] While her intent is to highlight the importance of what her interviewees do, she devalues, even ridicules, the environment—challenging as it might be—in which they work and choose to call home.

Scaffidi's surprise and discomfort is suggestive of what Roxanne Lynn Doty describes as the "imperial encounter"—that is, "asymmetrical encounters in which one has been able to construct 'realities' that were taken seriously and acted upon and the other entity has been denied equal degrees or kinds of agency."[24] There is not necessarily the "intention and calculations" to dominate or repress in this encounter—it is certainly the case that this was not Scaffidi's or any other Slow Food writer's intention—but rather the "taken-for-granted assumptions" about the "other."[25] These assumptions are, for Scaffidi, that she asks the questions, that she does not relinquish her position as the Western Slow Food authority and, lastly, that the Slow Food nominees have limited choice in determining where they settle and work. The reality is, as Scaffidi herself should be aware, that many Award nominees have made deliberately chosen to settle where they have. Many have studied abroad and returned to their villages or have opted to live in places where their skills would be most valuable to their people or country. To imply that the nominees have little choice in where they live or work is to deny them agency in what they do.

By resisting the possibility of dialog between herself and her interviewee, Scaffidi maintains her position of power and fails to disrupt the construction of the colonial "other" in Western culture as a subject without voice and without agency. These are just some examples of how Slow Food unwittingly reinforces an imperialist dichotomization of the Western self and its "other"—civilized and underdeveloped, powerful and powerless, generous benefactor and unfortunate beneficiary—while, like the Benetton ads, leaving the Slow Food reader with the sense that his or her membership fee is going to a "good cause."

The Class Issue
: :

I now wish to return to Chrzan, Laudan, Labelle and Gaytán to examine the relationship between Slow Food USA and its cultural "other" which is constituted not through racial difference but through an understanding of class in which European culture is held up as a pinnacle of culinary culture and sophistication, a "benchmark of superior lifestyle and consumption practices," whereby even the underprivileged are to be envied for their more traditional lives, their authenticity and for their diets of high-quality, artisanally produced food (Gaytán 2004: 113).[26] The sentimentalization of the European peasant is not dissimilar to the imperial nostalgia described by Rosaldo. Among convivium members in Slow Food USA, the failure to understand the part that privilege plays in feeding nostalgia leads to, as

Gaytán (2004: 113) identifies, "missed opportunities of political intervention within the realm of consumption." Convivium members turn to the European artisanal peasant whose cultural heritage and artisanal practices will save them from the tyranny of homogeneity imposed upon them by very same economic system that has bestowed them their privilege.

Chrzan, Laudan, Labelle and Gaytán each raise the issue of privilege in Slow Food's membership, which they argue limits Slow Food's relevance beyond those who have the luxury of philosophizing about matters of taste and diversity. Chrzan questions the high cost of many Slow Food activities, which are inaccessible to the broader population, and which from her own experience tend to prefer sharing high-quality food with like-minded people over discussing strategies for creating greater equity in the food system (Chrzan 2004: 123). Labelle, examining the organization's potential in formulating an alternative and more holistic approach to connecting the worlds of food production and consumption, similarly observes that Slow Food suffers from a failure to recognize that locally sourced produce and high-quality foods are luxuries for a privileged few. Labelle points out that, despite the organization's well-meaning agenda to protect cultural diversity, there appears to be little socio-economic diversity within its own membership, suggesting that Slow Food "might benefit from greater openness and encouragement of internal diversity" (Labelle 2004: 92). Laudan launches a similar attack against Slow Food in her scathing review of Petrini's *A Case for Taste*, arguing that his preachy condemnation of the modern food supply fails to consider the reality of the working poor for whom industrial, preprepared foods offer a relief from the "tyranny of the local" (Laudan 2004: 143).

Slow Food has in fact attempted to respond publicly to claims of elitism that have dogged the movement since its inception:

> Slow Food has never been and has no intention of becoming an elite movement. On the contrary, one of its principles is to ensure the right of pleasure to all ... Today, irrespective of social class, a great family of consumers attributes an added value to food, an anthropological surplus made up of cultural identity, the right to health, sensory pleasure, social relations and an improved quality of life.[27]

The principle of pleasure as a right for all is noble, yet the argument above somehow fails to hold water. Undoubtedly many would benefit from eating better, eating less or eating together more regularly but whether the pleasure offered by the "anthropological surplus" of food bears any relevance to a "great family of consumers" is questionable. After all, an anthropological surplus necessitates a preexisting surplus—of food, social access, leisure time and financial security—that is far from irrespective of class. While Slow

Food strives for inclusion in its understanding of pleasure as a right for all, it idealistically overlooks, or perhaps simply fails to grasp, how class is one of the most critical factors in differentiating who has access to this "surplus" and who does not. It is clear that the issue of elitism cannot be ignored either at the international level or amongst the convivium members interviewed by Gaytán who appear remarkably out of touch with the realities of the working class.[28] As Gaytán's interviewees attempt to envisage a better food future, their privilege manifests itself in a strong sense of nostalgia for disappearing cultural practices of Europe which reveals a critical lack of engagement with historical, economic or political issues that shape contemporary food culture in the US and the global food supply today.

Longing for the Past

Unfortunately many of the convivium members from northern California reinforce the stereotype of the well-heeled, wine-sipping Slow Food elite who have the good fortune of opting in or out of the global food supply, buying from the local farmers' market one day and enjoying artisanal European cheeses the next. In their privileged quest for access to the anthropological surplus of food, many reflect upon an age gone by when things were better. They long for a culture that understood the meaning of pleasure and in which the "lower classes," as one Slow Food member puts it, were "an artisan class." This mythical culture is constituted in contrast to contemporary American culture where "you have poor people without the artisan background" (Gaytán 2004: 112). The problem, according to another interviewee, is that "there is no peasant food in America. In other cultures, in Italy, there's polenta and pasta and things that are inexpensive and easy to make and Americans don't have peasant food" (Gaytán 2004: 112). Chrzan also touches on the use of nostalgia in Slow Food's efforts to create new markets in the US for traditional products, such as unpasteurized cheeses, which rely on "explicit philosophical ties to the native and regional cheese industries of Europe—the very cheeses that the European convivia seek to preserve" (Chrzan 2004: 124). The European peasant offers relief from the perceived "cultural adhedonia" of American culture for those who can afford it.

There are at least two problems with this idealized and sentimental understanding of Europe and its cultural and economic history. The first is the misperception that the dependence of peasant communities on basic staples such as polenta, often to their nutritional detriment, was determined by choice rather than by poverty (Laudan 2004: 136). Laudan has been highly critical of Slow Food's dogged privileging of the traditional over the modern, which she argues is underpinned by the misguided assumption that peasant food was somehow better quality, easier to prepare or more nutritious than food today (Laudan 2001, 2004). The second, more disturbing problem arises from the reasons articulated by the various interviewees for the ostensible absence of a rich and diverse food culture in the US: the underemphasis of taste, the ascetic denial of pleasure, the lack of an artisanal class and the loss of the traditional family values to hold a food culture together. They fail to recognize the conditions of inequity or oppression often inherent within the preservation of tradition—whether they are socio-economic differences limiting access to education and opportunity or a gender tradition in which the labor of women in the kitchen bears the responsibility for maintaining harmony in the family home and preserving the cultural traditions of society.

Both Gaytán and Chrzan express concern for the lack of any significant engagement with food policy. As Gaytán observes, by constantly referring back to a cultural and geographic locale beyond their own, these Slow Food communities reveal a global view that is fundamentally informed by the privilege of travel and education. As citizens of one of the most privileged nations in the world, the members of Slow Food USA are to some degree the beneficiaries of the global economy and have, as Laudan points out, "already reaped the benefits of Culinary Modernism" (Laudan 2004: 143). Yet, clouded by nostalgia, their outward-looking gaze remains blind to the economic and political structures in the global food supply that create economic disparity and restrict access to high quality food for a majority of consumers in their own country.

There is nothing fundamentally wrong with the pursuit of pleasure, nor with the desire to preserve the world's cultural and ecological diversity. What is really at question here is how Slow Food, whether in the US or Europe, goes about achieving this. Petrini is right to draw a parallel between the imperial expansion of the last 500 years and the ongoing problems of lack of food sovereignty around the world.[29] He also acknowledges that the future of gastronomy is nothing without an ethic that involves a discipline of the mind, a questioning of the self and, most importantly, an understanding of how one is positioned in the distribution of resources:

> The gastronome, if that means a passive beneficiary of agricultural resources and the wealth they generate, is yesterday's man, his ethic of profit and enjoyment compromised by the very world that legitimates him. Lacking a sense of responsibility toward both our alimentary heritage and its future users, and an awareness of the ethical choices that this heritage imposes, he has no future. Today the paradox of pleasure is the discipline you have to impose on yourself in pursuit of it, and the variety of forms that it can assume.[30]

An uncritical and nostalgic approach to the disappearance of traditions in other cultures does little to challenge the logic of imperialism that has shaped the exploitative nature of global capitalism. More than seeking to protect the traditions of others, an ethics of taste should produce a relation between the self and the "other" that is not only outward looking as it reaches out to this "other" but is simultaneously reflective and capable of questioning the self, its privilege and its assumptions. Only through a process of self-reflection can the relation between the inside and the outside become meaningful and go beyond a nostalgic rendering or fetishistic consumption of cultural diversity.

The Next Phase for Slow Food

: :

Despite its tendency towards sometimes problematic nostalgia, it is the organization's privilege and its knack for securing funding through membership fees and corporate and government sponsorship that enables Slow Food's growing influence in international circles. After almost two decades of focusing on the protection of culinary diversity of Europe, the international office of Slow Food is now entering a new phase. In the past five years the organization has dropped its annual fee significantly for members in developing nations, gained recognition as a non-governmental organization by the Food and Agricultural Organization and expanded the number of Presidia projects in Asia, Africa and the Americas.[31] In October 2004, Slow Food undertook its most ambitious initiative to date—Terre Madre: World Meeting of Food Communities—an event that brought together 5,000 food producers from 131 countries around the world. The intent of this approach was to create connections within supply chains and between food communities so that producers, processors, distributors, educators and others could exchange ideas for addressing the problems that confront them.

The event has not been without controversy. The astonishing €2.6 million needed to fund Terre Madre was raised from a variety of sources, including the national office of Slow Food USA for which Chrzan has expressed some concerns, and the right-wing regional government of Piedmonte undoubtedly has its own political agenda of establishing Italy as the European center of gastronomic tourism.[32] Slow Food is demonstrating an amazing capacity to bring together and influence individuals from across the spectrum of global politics—from ministers in the Berlusconi government to Mikhail Gorbachev, Prince Charles and environmental activist Vandana Shiva—without compromising its position of the bigger issues of trade laws, genetic modification technology and agricultural subsidies. To create any meaningful dialogue between the right and the left is already a significant achievement, and establishing some common ground is often a first step in effecting political change.

In spite of the controversy around Terre Madre, the fact that the travel and accommodation costs of delegates from poorer nations were covered by Slow Food enabled the participation of many small-scale producers and processors who could not normally afford to attend in an event of this kind. As Francis Fru N'Gang, Assistant Director of the African Institute for Economic and Social Development, suggested during his address at Terre Madre, the event was a unique opportunity for the politicians and food producers of more economically powerful nations to hear the voices of those men and women rarely heard in the political arena—from farming communities in war-torn regions of Rwanda to nomadic sheep breeders of Central Asia—and others often forgotten in the more large-scale meeting of minds such as WTO summits or the Food and Agriculture Organisation's World Food Summit.[33] A breeder of rare pigs from Australia indicated that this was one of the strengths of the event. The diversity of perspectives represented meant that the workshops were not only intensely political, but also challenged the trade, production and consumption practices of the world's richest nations. In this sense, Terre Madre was an opportunity to exchange ideas with others who share a commitment to protecting diversity in the food supply as well as a chance for the West to learn from communities for whom the fight to protect their food heritage is a question of survival.

In 2004, Slow Food signed an agreement to assist the Brazilian government in tackling the problem of hunger, which plagues one-third of the Brazilian population—or approximately 46 million people—despite the country being the fourth largest food exporter in the world. One of the key strategies of Zero Hunger is to move towards small-scale production and the cultivation of traditional crops—a policy very much aligned with Slow Food's philosophy—to increase food security, protect biodiversity and bolster the economies of local communities.[34] The agreement marks a unique opportunity for Slow Food to work cooperatively with a national government to effect change at a regional and national level in a country that possesses a significant portion of the world's cultural and ecological diversity.[35]

As a first step, the accord will set up four Presidia to support the small-scale production of traditional foods in Brazil. One of these Presidia is run by Obodias Battista Garcia, a chief of the Prié Mawé nation and an activist in the Amazonian indigenous movement, who allowed me to interview him via an interpreter while representing his guarana project at the Salone del Gusto. According to Maurizio Fabroni, a researcher and practitioner in social development, who established Presidia four years ago, the project is "a pioneer experiment involving an innovative model of economic development based on the preservation of a culture and of traditional knowledge, and on the safeguarding/appreciation of the heritage of biodiversity."[36] While Garcia had run the program for four years prior to

Fabroni's involvement, he said Slow Food has provided professional advice, valuable publicity and political support at an international level as well as the financial support to attend events such as Salone del Gusto and Terre Madre where he can exchange ideas with people undertaking similar projects. By developing national and international markets for guarana, the project also generates revenue for the Sateré Mawé to develop and implement social development programs for the local community. Savvy about the relationship between Slow Food and his people, Garcia is keenly aware of how these kinds of projects reflect favourably on Slow Food but, so long as they share mutual interests, he indicated that he would continue to work with Slow Food which "has a voice and gives weight to the issues" facing indigenous communities around the world.[37]

The undertaking of Terre Madre reflects an acknowledgement from Slow Food that defending the right to pleasure alone will never rectify the inequities of the global food supply. It also requires, as Frei Betto, head of Brazil's Zero Hunger program, stated in his address at Terre Madre, a defence of "the most elementary right: the right to eat."[38] It is clear that Slow Food will not single-handedly revolutionize the global food supply and that, just as Slow Food encourages consumers to be more attentive and thoughtful in the act of eating, likewise it needs to demonstrate a more critical use of nostalgia and greater attentiveness to the subtle forces of imperialism in its activities. Despite its limitations, Slow Food demonstrates enormous potential to effect change by not only using its networks to exert influence at an international level and by supporting grassroots activism such as Garcia's project, but also to bring the two together through events such as Terre Madre. Slow Food's success in the future will not be determined by the scale of its membership or its recognition in the popular press but by the creativity and autonomy that materializes from the projects it supports and by its capacity to campaign internationally for the social, environmental and political issues confronting communities such as the Sateré Mawé and others threatened by the effects of global capitalism in their regions.

The challenge for Slow Food is to recognize its own heritage of privilege derived from an economic system shaped by imperialism and to actively resist nostalgic renderings of the "other," however well intentioned, which fetishize cultural difference and sentimentalize struggles for cultural or economic survival. This requires more meaningful dialog between Slow Food and those it seeks to support in order to create a space of mutual respect and recognition of difference. As Christopher Falzon writes, dialog enables "a mutual interplay between the participants, as opposed to a one-way imposition of one upon the other," which necessitates "an attitude of openness towards the other, being open to different perspectives and to ways of acting which challenge the prevailing … social arrangements" and which create the conditions for "social transformation."[39] Slow Food needs to ensure that, in working towards an ethics of taste, the voices of those who are exploited by global capitalism are able to speak back to Slow Food—that is, to challenge its methods, to question assumptions and to ask, "¿Y vos?"

Notes

1. Slow Food, "Structure—Manifesto." Slow Food website; available from http://www.slowfood.com/eng/sf_cose/sf_cose_statuto.lasso (accessed October 12, 2003).
2. Petrini (2001: xxiii–xxiv).
3. Petrini (2001: 216–17).
4. Rosaldo (1989: 69).
5. Jones *et al.* (2003: 303).
6. Laudan (2001: 36).
7. Leitch (2003: 454).
8. Wilson and Dissanayake (1996: 9).
9. Rosaldo (1989: 70).
10. Dirlik (1996: 32).
11. Probyn (1999: 224).
12. Petrini (2003).
13. Petrini (2001: 23).
14. hooks (1992: 25).
15. hooks (1992: 23).
16. hooks (1992: 26).
17. Petrini (2001: 21).
18. hooks (1992: 21).
19. hooks (1992: 21).
20. Petrini (2000: 9).
21. Scaffidi (2003: 117).
22. Scaffidi (2003: 117.
23. Scaffidi (2003: 117.
24. Doty (1996: 3).
25. Doty (1996: 24).
26. It should also be noted that "Europe" appears to be constructed primarily through French and Italian culture but applied across the entire European continent without regard for the cultural differences that exist within and between European nations.
27. Slow Food Press Office, available from http://www.slowfood.com/eng/sf_stampa/sf_stampa.lasso (accessed February 19, 2004).
28. I do not wish to suggest that the views expressed in northern California are representative of all Slow Food members across the country or that there is malice in their intentions. Their comments merely serve as an example of how easy it is to slip into an uncritical use of nostalgia that romanticizes the hardship of others.
29. Petrini (2000).
30. Petrini (2001: 109–110).

31 Slow Food Press Office, "Slow Food Presidia Agreement with Brazil," July 23, 2004, http://www.slowfood.com/eng/sf_stampa/sf_stampa_dett_comu.lasso?idstampa=US_00311 (accessed August 18, 2004).

32 Hooper (2004).

33 N'Gang (2004).

34 Croce (2003: 4).

35 "Brazil's Food Security Policy—Hunger Zero", Website, http://www.pt.org.br/site/assets/cartilhas_ fomezero/Security%20Policy%20OK.pdf (accessed January 12, 2004).

36 Maurizio Fabroni, "Workshop 3: Traditional Knowledge And Management Of Natural Resources: ACOPIAMA—Scientific Committee and General Council of the SatereMawe Nation, Brazil," *Fighting Poverty: Social Innovations and New Coalitions*, July 25–27, 2000. (Eschborn: Deutsche Gesellschaft für Technische Zusammenarbeit, 2001): 128, http://www2.gtz.de/forum_armut/ GlobalDialogue/Documentation.pdf (accessed January 12, 2004).

37 Obodias Battista Garcia, chief of the Satare Mawe nation, interview with author, Torino, Italy, October 23, 2004.

38 Frei Betto, "Terre Madre—Zero World Hunger," *Sloweb*, November 18, 2004, http://www.slowfood.com/ eng/sf_sloweb/sf_arch_sloweek.lasso?-database=sf_sloweb&-layout=tutti&-response=sf_sloweb_dettaglio. lasso&-recordID=35577&-search (accessed January 12, 2004).

39 Falzon (1998: 7–8).

References

CHRZAN, J. 2004. Slow Food: What, Why, and to Where? *Food, Culture, and Society* 7(2): 117–132.
CROCE, P. DI. 2003. Slow Food and Lula: Presidia on the Brazilian Government Agenda. Slow 41:4.
DIRLIK, A. 1996. The Global in the Local. R. Wilson and W.Dissanayake (eds) *Global/Local: Cultural Production and the Transnational Imaginary*, pp. 21–45. Durham, NC: Duke University Press.
DOTY, R. L. 1996. *Imperial Encounters: The Politics of Representation in North-South Relations*. Minneapolis, MN: University of Minnesota Press.
FALZON, C. 1998. *Foucault and Social Dialogue: Beyond Fragmentation*. New York: Routledge.
GAYTÁN, M. S. 2004. Globalizing Resistance: Slow Food and New Local Imaginaries. *Food, Culture, and Society* 7(2): 97–116.
HOOKS, B. 1992. Eating the Other: Desire and Resistance. b. hooks (ed.) *Black Looks: Race and Representation*. Boston, MA: South End Press.
HOOPER, J. 2004. Peasant farmers of the world unite! *Guardian*, 20 October, http://www.guardian.co.uk/g2/story/0,3604,1331144,00.html.
JONES. P., SHEARS P., HILLIER, D., COMFORT, D. and LOWELL, J. 2003 Return to Traditional Values? A Case Study of Slow Food. *British Food Journal* 105: 297–304.
LABELLE, J. 2004. A Recipe for Connectedness: Bridging Production and Consumption with Slow Food. *Food, Culture, and Society* 7(2): 81–96.
LAUDAN, R. 2001. A Plea for Culinary Modernism: Why We Should Love New, Fast, Processed Food. *Gastronomica: the Journal of Food and Culture* 1(1): 36–44.
LAUDAN, R. 2004. Slow Food, the French Terroir Strategy, and Culinary Modernism: An Essay Review. *Food, Culture, and Society* 7(2): 133–149.
LEITCH, A. 2003. Slow Food and the Politics of Pork Fat: Italian Food and European Identity, *Ethnos* 68(4): 437–462.
N'GANG, F. F. 2004. Terre Madre—The Centrality of Africa. *Sloweb*, November 26, http://www.slowfood.com/eng/sf_sloweb/sf_sloweb_dettaglio.lasso?passaswe= SW_01451.
PETRINI, C. 2000. FOREWORD. C. SCAFFIDI and C. KUMMER (eds) *Premio Slow Food* Bra: Slow Food Editore.

PETRINI, C. 2001. *Slow Food: Case for Taste*. New York: Columbia University Press.
PETRINI, C. 2003. Special Edition: Identity and Social Relations in New Rural Communities. *Sloweb,* July18, http://www.slowfood.com/eng/sf_sloweb/sf_arch_carlin.lasso?-database=sf_sloweb&-layout=tutti&-response=sf_sloweb_dettaglio.lasso&-recordID=34725&-search.
PROBYN, E. 1999. Beyond Food/Sex: Eating and an Ethics of Existence. *Theory, Culture and Society* 16: 215–228.
ROSALDO, R. 1989. Imperialist Nostalgia. R. Rosaldo (ed.) *Culture and Truth: The Remaking of Social Analysis*. Boston, MA: Beacon Press.
SCAFFIDI, C. 2003. ¿Y vos?. *Slow Ark* 1: 117.
WILSON, R. and DISSANAYAKE, W. 1996. Introduction: Tracking the Global/Local. R. Wilson and W. Dissanayake (eds) *Global/Local: Cultural Production and the Transnational Imaginary*, pp. 1–18. Durham, NC: Duke University Press.

Perspectives on Teaching

Kyla Wazana **Tompkins**
Pomona College

Literary Approaches to Food Studies

Eating the Other

In the syllabus that follows I outline a semester-long class that I taught at Pomona College in the fall of 2004. This course was cross-listed with the English Department and with the Program in Women's Studies, where I am jointly appointed. In the future it will also be listed as an American Studies course. I taught this class during my first semester at Pomona in response to the student interest in food studies that was shown during my job talk and campus visit the spring before. In fact the class was one of the first classes to be filled during pre-enrollment so interest was clearly very strong.

: :

At present my research looks at the relationship between racial and gender formation in the nineteenth-century US. In my book project "Stomaching Difference: Race, Food and the Body Politic in the Nineteenth-Century US," I demonstrate that eating has long functioned as a cultural trope for the encounter with racial and social difference in the literary and visual culture of the US. Building on this research, in this course I aim to complicate the work of structuralist anthropologists and folklorists including Mary Douglas, Roland Barthes and Levi Strauss, all of whom persuasively demonstrate that food is a communicative medium; I do so by demonstrating that food consistently disrupts written text as a sign of embodied existence, as a mark of the outer limits of language, and as a trope for written language's inability to fully represent the life of the body. This reading of food-language as signifying the constitutive outside of textuality in turn demonstrates that food and eating function as privileged sites for the representation of racial and ethnic difference in the West, where racial difference is consistently signified both through vernacular (or hyper-embodied) language and through liminally human or extra-social (lower-body) physicality. The close relationship between Western food desires and the history of colonialism and imperialism in turn serve both to underline and historically constitute these connections.

This course was meant to provide background to students more broadly interested in food studies and literature, leading up to the explosion in food culture that took place between the 1980s and the end of the century. I gave my course the title "Eating the Other" after the essay by Black feminist critic, bell hooks, who wrote:

> ... the commodification of difference promotes paradigms of consumption wherein whatever difference the Other inhabits is eradicated, via exchange, by a consumer cannibalism that not only displaces the Other but denies the significance of that Other's history through a process of decontextualization. (hooks 1992)

In this quote hooks points to the consumption of racial and ethnic difference as a hallmark of bourgeois identity; she also critically notes that this "consumer cannibalism" in essence devours the evidence and testimony of the history of inequality. In doing so it erases the full historical subjectivity of the subject it consumes; eating here becomes the desiring and destructive mode through which otherness is both encountered and destroyed.

The underlying narrative of this syllabus is here expressed through seven critical approaches that I want my students to bring to every text. This list is not meant to be exhaustive but rather descriptive of my own particular research and pedagogical interests. I list them here:

1. Every food discourse or representation has a relationship to a specific body politic. That is, food is a way of talking about the body, of constructing both ideal and abject social bodies. In literature this happens through the representation of consumption in literary texts as well as through implicit assumptions about the body and what fuels it. Studying food thus becomes one mode of learning medical history, particularly when studying those periods and cultures, like antebellum America or ancient Greece, in which food and medicine are often seen as the same thing.

2. Studying food in literature is one mode of studying material history. Thus it is particularly useful to pay attention to the food objects that are associated with particular social locations. In studying what kinds of food appear in literature we can trace the economic and cultural circuits that are in play during the moment of cultural production. For instance, in studying alcohol in nineteenth-century US literature we ask: how does the writer relate to widespread antebellum temperance activity? If the writer is discussing rum, a Caribbean alcohol made from plantation sugar, how might slavery form part of the novel's political unconscious?

3. Structuralist anthropologists use language systems to explain the ways in which we make meaning through food: in their work food is described as a system of communication. Food and language are often collapsed in this body of work; for instance, food and the meal are formally compared to forms of literature, including poems. Beyond a purely social reading, this phenomenon has what we might term a physical explanation: both food and speech are experienced in the mouth. However, it is significant that both communicative systems—if we wish to read them as analogous—are sites where there is particular cross-border cultural movement: the transnational economic and cultural relationships organized around food change "domestic" languages by importing new vocabularies along with new cuisines. Thus food consistently signals to the borders of what we might term national bodies and thus to the ruptures in the borders of both

nation and body that are marked by what comes into and goes out of the mouth.

4. Reaching back to Plato's Symposium, there is a historical relationship between food, meals and philosophical discourse, but also food, meals and storytelling. Meals structure narrative and vice versa.

5. There is a history of food symbols that we find in the Old and New Testament in which eating is consistently represented as a metaphor for the taking in of knowledge or for learning. This relationship in turn sets up a parallel between words and food: words become food and "bibliophagy" is often encoded in literary texts about food.

6. Eating is also a mode through which we exceed our individuality and join with others: forms of commensality and communion join disparate individuals both to each other and to the realm of the spiritual. Food rules and covenants are thus often a way of joining the self and the community to God, either by following law or through sacrifice (pouring libations) or both.

7. There is a metaphorics of eating that represents what we might think of as a fundamental epistemological binary in our world: the division between a structuring body's "inside" and "outside." Taking the boundaries of the body as a fundamental heuristic tool, eating thus comes to be understood as an important metaphor for social and political difference.

Taking these seven points as an argumentative beginning, my goals in this course were both diachronic and synchronic: I wanted to offer both a historical perspective on food in literature and to use this history to contextualize certain issues in contemporary food culture. At the risk of sounding clichéd, I wanted to pass on my own fascination with food culture; I also wanted to defamiliarize what is often an unquestioned aspect of everyday life, thus using food studies as an exercise in critical approaches to the social and cultural world. Too often, fluency in food culture, like being "well-read" or "well-traveled," is a sign of a certain privileged bourgeois cosmopolitanism: in my course understanding food on a deeper level means also paying attention to the sometimes rather bloody and visceral issues that lurk behind an otherwise pleasant topic.

In retrospect, my own desire to problematize eating and the class relations that lurk behind consumption led to mixed responses from the class. In part, this is because of the very mixed bag of students that I had, all of whom seemed to have different desires for the course. For some, food studies clearly signaled a "fun" course (read: easy). These students were invariably disappointed with the amount of reading I gave them and in particular they got mad when I asked them to read cultural theory. I also had a contingent of science students fulfilling breadth requirements who were new and at times very resistant to reading theory.

On the other hand, I also had a very politicized group of students coming out of women's studies who enjoyed reading theory and often dominated the conversations in which we problematized the power relations that lurk behind representations of food and eating. Those students seemed to conflict with my purely literary students who were far more interested in performing close literary readings and wanted to discuss esthetics; it is not that the latter resisted politicized readings but they did resist purely political readings.

This *olla podrida* of students made the large class somewhat difficult to please at all times, but it also often produced interesting differences of opinion; Pomona students are not shy with their opinions generally and some very productive disagreements took place. For instance, during the reading of Marya Hornbacher's anorexia novel *Wasted*, a group of students felt that Hornbacher's self-starvation was problematic in view of larger issues of global starvation. Operating from an identitarian politic, they were critical of Hornbacher's confessional narrative of suffering given her class status. Other students, some of whom later confessed to me that they themselves were former anorexics or bulimics, felt that her class status was immaterial in view of the idea that eating disorders are diseases and thus, in a sense, outside of global power narratives. Still others wanted to read bulimia and anorexia as textual issues; given Hornbacher's stated desire to "write the body into text," her manic, at times Jamesian, sentences were clearly of formal interest.

Navigating these disciplinary lobby groups proved to be interesting work during my first semester as a teacher, to say the least. At first I found disagreement in the classroom to be stressful, including political disagreements: a major lesson for me as a new teacher that semester was to trust students to deal with differences of opinion and not try to smooth them over. This included those students who came in office hours to ask me to advocate particular political positions: instead I tried to foster mutual respect without advocating particular points of view. This approach led to various fits of undergraduate grumpiness but it also called on students to be responsible for their own positions in classroom discussion.

Another point of resistance was to reading popular "women's" novels like Joanne Harris' *Chocolat* and Laura Esquivel's *Like Water for Chocolate*. Granted, I did assign these novels during "easy" weeks at the end of the semester, however my larger goal in assigning those texts was to ask students to problematize contemporary popular food discourses. I have found that students sometimes resist reading "popular" texts in literature classes. This, it seems to me, is very much a leftover of the history of English departments themselves, as spaces of "civility" and class indoctrination. English students sometimes expect to read Great Works in English classes: reading popular twentieth-century novels got some of them very irritated. However, in my teaching and research I am very committed to a building upon a David Reynolds-ian approach to literary and cultural studies. I want students to consider the popular literature of a period not only because it was popular and thus a window into the interests of large swaths of population but also because doing so opens up conversations about the construction of literary canons and educational curricula. These last two novels, in all of their purple and delicious glory, are very much representative of a certain genre of "food porn" literature that emerged in the bourgeois food crazes of the last two decades of the twentieth century. Interrogating the political unconscious of this kind of literature was one of the central goals of the course. We had some really great conversations about popular fiction and its cultural work during these weeks and the easier texts also allowed some of the less confident students to speak up with more confidence.

In assigning those books and films, I also wanted students to think about the connections between older texts, like Rabelais' *Gargantua* and Plato's *Symposium*, to contemporary ways of thinking about eating, consumption and pleasure. Plato's *Symposium* which takes place after a dinner has concluded, and is thus a text that segregates philosophical conversation from eating—eating being a concern of the body and philosophy a concern of the soul. However, Plato does link philosophy to wine—the entire cast of characters is, in fact, hung over during the conversation. And it is Alcibiades' disruptive and drunken entrance into the Symposium that poses the fundamental disjunct of the text, between platonic, spiritual existence and an existence structured around the (lower, sexual, digestive) needs of the (lower, sexual, digestive) body. In fact following on Francois Jeanneret's wonderful book *Feast of Words*, we read the first book of Rabelais' *Gargantua* as a response to just such symposiac literature. In these terms, *Gargantua* is a text that engages the lower body in such a way as to be generative of philosophical discourse: in Rabelais one does not live a life in spite of the body, but rather, *through* the body.

Two texts that students particularly enjoyed reading were Verta Mae Grosvenor's *Vibration Cooking* and Monique Truong's *The Book of Salt*. The explicit themes of race and postcoloniality spoke directly to the larger class content and tied food culture to the performance and delineation of ethnic identity. The class was seriously split on John Lancaster's *Debt to Pleasure*, given its utterly unlikeable narrator, Tarquin Winot. However Lancaster's portrayal of gourmandism as murder led to some of the best literary readings of the semester, in which students considered the ethical stakes of esthetic criticism as a mode of delineating Bourdieuvian class *distinction*. Another interesting reading emerged in which we discussed taste as a form of solipsism and thus as an inroad into talking about the homicidal and very unreliable narrator. If taste is a solipsistic sense, what are social standards of taste but fiction? This line of questioning proved particularly useful in light of Lancaster's former career as a restaurant critic, driving us to ask if criticism is itself a form of murder. Thus while many students initially disliked the text intensely, a surprising number of them wrote final papers on Lancaster's novel.

Another text that excited students was Morgan Spurlock's documentary *Super Size Me*. Many students in the class found Spurlock's consistent use of African American subjects as representative bodies appalling in view of the film's lack of race analysis. This, in concert with the centrality of his own (very) white body, led the class to dub the film *Super Me*. Other students found the film persuasive and important, and admired Spurlock for taking on McDonald's. I admit to setting Spurlock up a bit by scheduling the film during the same week as Hornbacher's memoir of her eating disorder, *Wasted*, but was really surprised by the intensity with which students disliked the film.

Although I suppose it could be classified as a "popular" novel, students adored Ruth Ozeki's *My Year of Meats* as a text through which to discuss globalization, gender politics and the still-open question of America's global cultural hegemony. Returning to Sidney Mintz's essay, we also spent some time discussing the question of whether there is such a thing as American cuisine, explored Ozeki's linking of sexual politics, reproduction and agribusiness, and discussed the ethics of eating meat. In the end, students were ambivalent about the novel's representation of a Japanese woman who finds 'freedom in the US, as well as the novel's sometimes surfactory treatment of racial and geographic diversity. This thematically rich, if somewhat imperfect, novel was one of the most useful texts we read all semester.

The least successful week, without doubt, was the week on postcoloniality and cannibalism. Although I found myself fascinated with Nelson Pereira Dos Santos' *How Tasty Was My Frenchman*, students found the Brazilian *Cinema Novo* esthetic uninspiring. To my surprise we also had a hard time that week tying together De Montaigne with Dos Santos and the Brazilian surrealist Retamar's manifesto. That, without a doubt, was my fault and I'll either cut that week and shift or limit the readings next time. The topic of cannibalism as I presented it in that week was too far afield from the rest of the class and it will take some paring down and focusing to make it work next time.

Students also had negative, though very engaged, responses to Peter Greenaway's *The Cook, The Thief, The Wife and Her Lover*, as well as Anthony Bourdain's *Kitchen Confidential*. Once again, both texts produced engaged and very interesting papers.

In terms of the classroom work itself, I gave short lectures and led class discussions on Tuesdays and organized students into weekly panels on

Thursdays. This is a teaching technique that I borrowed from a teacher of mine at the University of Toronto, Professor Linda Hutcheon, and it is designed to both provoke conversation and give students practice in public speaking. Each student participated in two of these panels over the course of the semester, in which they gave a one-page position paper or close reading of the text of the week. They then produced two short papers in which they took the weekly discussion into account. This took a lot of modeling and coaching: I provided a sample one-page paper with discussion questions at the beginning of the class. However I do think that this is actually quite useful as an exercise because it encourages students to work together and, more important, to speak to each other. For those students who go on to graduate school it provides an early model for later professionalization.

Finally, each panel was required to bring in a "food of the week." During the week on cannibalism, we ate Sour Patch Kids; during the chocolate weeks I brought in ten-pound blocks of chocolate from Ghirardelli. During the week we discussed Hornbacher, students brought in gum, according to the author a favorite food of anorexics. During the week that we discussed the Terezin concentration camp cookbook, *In Memory's Kitchen*, students brought nothing.

Syllabus

LITERATURE AND REFERENCE BOOKS

- Sharon Tyler Herbst, *The New Food Lover's Companion*.
- Rabelais, *Gargantua and Pantagruel*.
- Vertamae Smart-Grosvenor, *Vibration Cooking*.
- Ruth Ozeki, *My Year of Meats*.
- Marya Hornbacher, *Wasted: A Memoir of Anorexia and Bulimia*.
- Laura Esquivel, *Like Water for Chocolate*.
- Monica Truong, *Salt*.
- Anthony Bourdain, *Kitchen Confidential*.
- John Lancaster, *The Debt to Pleasure*.
- Cara De Silva, *In Memory's Kitchen*.
- Joanne Harris, *Chocolat*.

FILMS

- Morgan Spurlock's *Super Size Me*.
- Eddie Murphy's *The Nutty Professor*.

- Peter Greenaway's *The Cook, The Thief, His Wife and Her Lover.*
- Nelson Pereira dos Santos, *How Tasty Was My Little Frenchman.*
- Lasse Hallstrom's *Chocolat.*

WEEK ONE—INTRODUCTIONS

Lesson one—Syllabus Introduction. Discussion: Julia Kristeva, excerpt from the *Powers of Horror: An Essay on Abjection* (Kristeve 1982)

Lesson two—Claude Levi-Strauss "The Culinary Triangle"; "Raw Food" introduction to *Raw: The Cookbook* (Trotter and Klein 2004).

In week one I introduce the students to reading food literature critically and to understanding some of the theoretical underpinnings of food studies. On the first day we go through a paragraph from feminist critic Julia Kristeva's discussion of the skin of milk in her essay on abjection and the creation of the self in order to start thinking about the body as a template for constructing social relations. We begin to think through a basic metaphorics of "inside" and "outside" to understand social hierarchy and belonging, and we discuss abjection, disgust and horror as seemingly physiological responses that are intertwined with a political metaphorics of disgust.

On the second day we read the introduction to Charlie Trotter and Roxanne Klein's cookbook with Levi Strauss's "Culinary Triangle" to understand how both texts naturalize social difference through their construction of "primitive" and "developed" foodways. In the former text, particularly, we read Klein's philosophical/autobiographical piece with an eye to class and body politics: drawing on a comparison with "Eskimo" foodways, Klein argues that eating raw food essentially returns the body to an originary natural state. At the same time she uses the language of modernity to describe the effects of the raw food diet: the body becomes efficient and energized, is able to exercise more, and so forth. We use these images to begin to discuss food discourses as markers of social difference.

WEEK TWO—EATING AS METAPHOR/READING FOOD AS A TECHNIQUE OF SOCIAL DIFFERENTIATION

Lesson one—Kilgour (1990); Fussell (1993).

Lesson two—Old Testament: Genesis 1–4; 25: 19–34; 27: 1–30; selections from Leviticus. New Testament: Matthew 26: 1–29; Mark 14: 1–25

In week two we use Betty Fussell's short story to explore Maggie Kilgour's important essay on metaphors of incorporation. Building on deconstructivist, feminist and postcolonial theory, as well as close readings of classic and early modern texts, Kilgour explores eating—that is, the incorporation of foreign elements into the body—as a metaphor through which the idea of otherness is both represented and consumed (and thus rendered fictive).

Betty Fussell's story takes up the biblical food images that we explore in the next lesson: Eve's consuming of the fruit of the knowledge of good and evil; the representation of the snake as Satan, but also as forbidden food; and the presentation of various religious food laws including the Hebrew injunction not to take life, and thus not to eat blood. By embracing the abject, in particular the blood, guts and innards of the eel, the narrator of Fussell's story exploits this biblical imagery in order to politicize female labor, revealing the kitchen as a fraught domestic space.

In another part of the lesson, we read two different renditions of the last supper as a way into discussing Kilgour's notion of the communion as a metaphor for the conjoining of self with community, the sacred with the mundane.

WEEK THREE—FIRST COURSE, DIS/COURSE: HOW TO READ A MEAL
::

Lesson one—Roland Barthes, "Toward A Psychosociology of Contemporary Food Consumption" (Barthes 1997); Mary Douglas, "Deciphering A Meal" (Douglas 1997).

Lesson two—panel presentation; Steingarten (2002). Mintz (2002).

This week introduces students to the notion that the meal is a cultural text in and of itself, which can be read formally—through the differential relationships between their separate parts—and in terms of the larger narratives of national/cultural identity that surround it. Through Jeffrey Steingarten's articles we discuss food fears and the social borders that these phobias both reveal and bolster. We then discuss the notion/problematic of a national American cuisine: does it exist, what does it look like? Can a national cuisine be defined by heterogeneity, speed and industrialized food? What border does the idea of a national cuisine protect? What borders does the meal contain? What food rules do we obey?

WEEK FOUR—NONSENSE, THE VERNACULAR AND THE DISCOURSE OF THE LOWER BODY
::

Lesson one—Rabelais's *Gargantua* (Book One) (Rabelais 1990).

Movie: excerpt from Eddie Murphy's performance in *The Nutty Professor*, in particular the family dinner scene.

Lesson two—panel presentation; Jeanneret (1987): Introduction and Chapter 5.

Week four explores the idea that representing the life of the body disrupts written language; in this week however we also look at the overdetermined relationship between the body, minoritarian racial identities, and vernacular language. We do so through a comparison between Rabelais' *Gargantua*, the first novel to be written in French, and a outrageously bawdy dinner scene in Eddie Murphy's production of *The Nutty Professor*. In these texts we look at the life of the lower body, at the idea that appetite is comic and base. We also explore the concept that the modern, post-Enlightenment subject is defined by a body that is contained with its own skin: a body, and thus a self, that is sealed. Those bodies that threaten to burst at the seams, that leak or are soft or that reveal orifices are thus seen as premodern, liminal or non-human social subjects, usually connected to the lower body. At the same time, these subjects' social status is undermined by their representation as *oral* or *vernacular*—speakers whose words are disrupted by their overdetermined physicality.

WEEK FIVE—FOOD AND THE ABJECT
::

Lesson one—Introduction to Stallybrass and White (1986); Grosvenor; (1970); Chapter 4 of *Uncle Tom's Cabin*.

Lesson two—panel presentation; slide show of late nineteenth-century trade card advertisements.

Week five continues the previous week's discussion with a closer look at the history of African-Americans in the food culture of the US. We examine the representation of African-American women as edible objects in *Uncle Tom's Cabin* and then look at Verta Mae Grosvenor's groundbreaking cookbook as a defense and celebration of African-American foodways. In particular we look at her rescuing of otherwise abject food items such as chitterlings ("chitlins"), possum, and bear and discuss what it means to take up the social space of abjection as a liberatory, antiracist strategy.

Borrowing from my book project, we also read Chapter 4 of *Uncle Tom's Cabin* alongside postbellum trade card advertisements that depict African Americans as edible objects. Using Stallybrass and White we seek to understand the complex intermingling of desire and disgust that characterizes relations of inequality and intimacy in the US.

WEEK SIX—RACE, CANNIBALISM AND THE POSTCOLONIAL

Lesson one—De Montaigne (1993); De Andrade (1992); Retamar (1989).

Movie: Nelson Pereira Dos Santos' *How Tasty Was My Little Frenchman*.

Thursday, October 7—panel presentation.

Week six looks at the connections between colonialism and cannibalism in the Renaissance period with the writings of De Montaigne and then discusses the revision of the trope of cannibalism as an anticolonial, nationalist symbol during the Brazilian Modernisto movement. We work through different interpretations of cannibalism as a strategy for maintaining the boundaries of group identity.

WEEK SEVEN—MEAT, SEX AND GENDER (ETHICS, INDUSTRIALIZATION, GLOBALIZATION)

Lesson one—Ozeki (1998).

Lesson two—panel presentation; "A Vegetarian Philosophy" from Singer (2000).

In week seven we debate the ethics of vegetarianism and discuss the social/species line between animal and human as constitutive of the definition of the category of "human." We look at Ruth Ozeki's treatment of sexual politics and globalization through the metaphorics of consuming meat in an era of multinational capitalism. We continue our discussion of cuisine as constitutive of national/cultural boundaries and extend that discussion to consider the strategies of cooptation and resistance that develop when multinational corporations transcend those borders in the service of neoliberal capitalism.

WEEK EIGHT—FAT BODIES, THIN BODIES AND DISORDERLY EATERS

Lesson one—Fall Recess.

Movie: *Super Size Me*

Lesson two—Marya Hornbacher's *Wasted*.

Week eight explores eating as a resistance strategy in eating-disordered women by putting an autobiography of a woman who survived multiple eating disorders in conversation with Morgan Spurlock's film *Super Size Me*. We discuss race and the body in the US, including Hornbacher's emulation of white, middle-class femininity and look at Spurlock's failure to address race and poverty as social problems that contribute to obesity. Finally we discuss the idea that this is a cultural moment fascinated with the plasticity of the body, with the body as one of the last frontiers to be conquered and tamed in the postmodern era.

WEEK NINE—ART, GENDER AND THE MEAL: THE RECIPISTOLARY NOVEL
::

Lesson one—Laura Esquivel's *Like Water for Chocolate*.

Lesson two—panel presentation; Leonardi (1989).

Week nine looks at what Doris Witt has called "recipistolary fiction," that is, at fiction that intersperses narrative with recipes. Usually marketed as women's novels, in this week we explore the semiotics of domesticity and of domestic space. Specifically, we talk about the literary possibilities inherent in the space of the kitchen, and at the ways in which different writers have represented the kitchen as a space of exploitation and repression at the same time as it is troped by the literary market as a site of sensual pleasure.

WEEK TEN—SEX, FOOD, ART AND SILENCE
::

Lesson one—selection from Toklas (1954); Truong (2003).

Lesson two—panel presentation.

Continuing the discussion of the kitchen as an important literary space, in this week we look at Monique Truong's novel/response to the *Alice B. Toklas Cookbook* alongside extracts from the cookbook that discuss the chefs who traversed the Stein/Toklas household. Reversing the previous discussion of the links between food and vernacular speech, in this week we look at the literary relationship between food and silence and at the kitchen as a foreign space within the domestic sphere. Finally, we examine two very different readings of the long relationship between Alice B. Toklas and Gertrude Stein.

WEEK ELEVEN—DISGUST, MASCULINITY AND THE KITCHEN
::

Lesson one—Bourdain (2000).

Movie: *The Cook, The Thief, The Wife and Her Lover*, Peter Greenaway.

Lesson two—panel presentation—Chapter 4 from Miller (1998).

Week eleven continues the investigation of the kitchen as a cultural space with a close look at two very masculine kitchens. In particular we investigate disgust as a cultural strategy through William Ian Miller's discussion of the social esthetics of disgust. How do these artists/writers negotiate gender in the kitchen through an esthetics of the abject? How does the kitchen become a space for the expression of an abject and aggressively masculine heteronormative sexuality? How do male kitchens differ from female kitchens?

WEEK TWELVE—ESTHETICISM: TASTE, CLASS, DISTINCTION
: :

Lesson one—Lancaster (1996).

Lesson two—panel presentation Chapter 3: "On Gastronomy" and Chapter 12: "On Gourmands" from Brillat-Savarin (1994).

Week twelve looks at criticism and food writing through two texts, one literary the other philosophical, which articulate social identity through distinction or class delineation. What is a gourmand? Is criticism (negation) an art form? What does Lancaster have to say about snobbery? How do "tastes" articulate identity? Are there modern corollaries of Brillat-Savarin's gourmand?

WEEK THIRTEEN—FOOD, HUNGER AND MEMORY
: :

Lesson one—Cara de Silva and the women of Terezin concentration camp. De Silva (1996).

Lesson two—Thanksgiving

Week thirteen investigates the creation, translation and reception of the Terezin cookbook. Flipping the order of things from the description of eating (the problem of explaining the senses) to the creation of art out of hunger, we examine the fragmentary nature of this book to further understand the problem of recreating/rewriting history. How did the women of Terezin articulate, defend and create group identity through food memory? Is it possible to comprehend the magnitude of those forms of hunger/suffering through these recipes?

WEEK FOURTEEN—CULINARY TOURISM: EATING THE OTHER

Lesson one—Harris (1999).

Movie: *Chocolat.*

Lesson two—panel presentation; Heldke (2003).

This last week is both a reprieve for the students as they prepare their final papers and a direct querying of the connections between bourgeois modes of food consumption, tourism and popular art. We discuss the history of chocolate as it was discovered and exported from the Americas after colonization, its connection to romance and sexuality and Harris's use of Aztec iconography to describe these cultural phenomena. Using Heldke's wonderful discussion of the relationship of food tourism to the fetishization of non-Western cultures, this last week focuses the student's attention on their own modes of consumption. Finally, Heldke's work directs students' attention to the ethics of eating in a global context.

References

BARTHES, R. 1997. Toward A Psychosociology of Contemporary Food Consumption. R Barthes *Food and Culture: A Reader*, pp. 20–27. New York: Routledge.
BOURDAIN, A. 2000. *Kitchen Confidential: Adventures in the Culinary Underbelly*. New York: HarperCollins.
BOURDIEU, P. 1984. *Distinction: A Social Critique of the Judgement of Taste*. Cambridge, MA: Harvard University Press, 1984.
BRILLAT-SAVARIN, J. 1994. "On Gastronomy"; Chapter 12: "On Gourmands". J. Brillat-Savarin *The Physiology of Taste*, pp. 141–154. New York: Penguin.
DE ANDRADE, O. 1992. The Cannibal Manifesto. *Exquisite Corpse: A Journal of Life and Letters* Spring/Summer, http://www.corpse.org/issue_11/manifestos/deandrade.html.
DE MONTAIGNE, M. 1993. On the Cannibals. M. De Montaigne *The Complete Essays*, pp. 228-240. New York: Penguin Classics.
DE SILVA, C. 1996. *In Memory's Kitchen*. Northvale, NJ: Jason Aronson Inc.
DOUGLAS, M. 1997. Deciphering A Meal. M. Douglas *Food and Culture: A Reader*, pp. 36–54. New York: Routledge.
ESQUIVEL, L. 1995. *Like Water for Chocolate*. New York: Random House.
FUSSELL, B. 1993. On Murdering Eels and Laundering Swine. B. Fussell *Not For Bread Alone*, pp. 120–124. Hopewell, NJ: The Ecco Press.
GROSVENOR, V. M. S. 1970. *Vibration Cooking, or the Travel Notes of a Geechee Girl*. New York: Doubleday.
HARRIS, J. 1999. *Chocolat*. New York: Penguin.
HELDKE, L. 2003. The Pursuit of Authenticity. L. Heldke *Exotic Appetites: Ruminations of A Food Adventurer*, pp. 23–44. New York: Routledge.
HERBST, S. T. 1995. *The New Food Lover's Companion*. 2nd edn. New York: Barron's Educational Series.
HOOKS, B. 1992. Eating the Other. *Black Looks: Race and Representation*. Toronto: Between the Lines Press.
HORNBACHER, M. 1998. *Wasted: A Memoir of Anorexia and Bulimia*. New York: HarperCollins.
JEANNERET, F. 1987. Introduction and Chapter 5 F. Jeanneret *A Feast of Words: Banquets and Table Talk in the Renaissance*. Chicago, IL: University of Chicago Press.
KILGOUR, M. 1990. Introduction. M. Kilgour *Communion to Cannibalism: Towards An*

Anatomy Of Metaphors Of Incorporation, pp. 3–19. Princeton, NJ: Princeton University Press.

KRISTEVA, J. 1982. *Powers of Horror: An Essay on Abjection*. trans. Leon S. Roudiez. New York: Columbia University Press.

LANCASTER, J. 1996. *The Debt to Pleasure*. New York: Picador.

LEONARDI, S. 1989. Recipes for Reading: Summer Pasta, Lobster a la Riseholme, and Key Lime Pie. *Publication of the Modern Language Association* 104(1): 340–347.

LEVI STRAUSS, C. The Culinary Triangle. C. Levi Strauss *Food and Culture: A Reader*, pp. 28–35. New York: Routledge,

MILLER, W. I. 1998. Chapter 4: "The Senses". W. Miller *The Anatomy of Disgust*, pp. 60–88. Cambridge, MA: Harvard University Press.

MINTZ, S. 2002. Eating American. S. Mintz *Food in the USA: A Reader*. New York: Routledge.

OZEKI, R. 1998. *My Year of Meats*. New York: Penguin Books.

PLATO. 1999. *Symposium*. Translation, Seth Benardete. Chicago, IL: University of Chicago Press.

RABELAIS, F. 1990. *Gargantua and Pantagruel*. New York: W.W. Norton & Company.

RETAMAR, R. F. 1989. *Caliban and Other Essays*, pp. 3–45. Minneapolis, MN: University of Minnesota Press.

REYNOLDS, D. 1988. *Beneath the American Renaissance: The Subversive Imagination in the Age of Imagination*. Cambridge, MA: Harvard University Press.

SINGER, P. 2000. A Vegetarian Philosophy. P Singer *Consuming Passions: Writings on An Ethical Life*. New York: Ecco Press.

STALLYBRASS, P. and WHITE, A. 1986. *The Politics and Poetics of Transgression*. Ithaca, NY: Cornell University Press..

STEINGARTEN, J. 2002. Why Doesn't Everyone In China Have A Headache, and Cheese Crise. J. Steingarten *It Must Have Been Something I Ate*. New York: Knopf.

STOWE, H. B. 1981. *Uncle Tom's Cabin Or, Life Among the Lowly*. New York: Penguin Books.

TOKLAS, A. 1954. Dishes for Artists, Murder in the Kitchen, and Servants in France. A. Toklas *The Alice B. Toklas Cookbook*. New York: Harper & Row.

TROTTER, C and KLEIN, R. 2004. *Raw: The Cookbook*. Berkeley, CA: Ten Speed Press..

TRUONG, M. 2003. *The Book of Salt*. New York: Houghton Mifflin.

WITT, D. 1999. *Black Hunger: Race and the Politics of US Identity*. New York: Oxford University Press.

Book Reviews

MANLY MEALS AND MOM'S HOME COOKING: COOKBOOKS AND GENDER IN MODERN AMERICA, by Jessamyn Neuhaus (Baltimore, MD: Johns Hopkins University Press, 2003).

Arising from Jessamyn Neuhaus' detailed examination of over 500 cookbooks alongside magazine "recipes and cooking tips," *Manly Meals and Mom's Home Cooking* illuminates the construction of middle-class domestic ideology through cookery instruction. As Neuhaus points out, the recipes and prescriptive lessons housed within a given cookbook "tell us less about the real, lived experience of women in the kitchen than about how cookbook producers imagined the ideal, 'normal' American home and the roles that men and women would play within it" (p. 4). Neuhaus convincingly demonstrates that these idealized versions worked to keep the middle-class wife bound to the stove and the husband away from daily meal preparation, a task so feminized it could emasculate even the most virile man.

Although *Manly Meals and Mom's Home Cooking* focuses primarily on the years 1920–1963, the first chapter begins with a whirlwind tour of written cookery instruction in eighteenth-century America, which largely comprised cookbooks imported from England. Throughout the remainder of the chapter, Neuhaus charts the development of a distinctly American cookbook tradition from Amelia Simmons' *American Cookery*, which appeared in 1796, up through World War I. This first chapter begins to suggest that *Manly Meals and Mom's Home Cooking* might benefit from a heavier reliance on footnotes to help weed the fact-saturated passages.

In her second chapter, Neuhaus begins the detailed examination of cookery instruction that makes her project a work of scholarly significance. To begin, she notes that during the 1920s and 1930s, industry yoked itself so successfully to home economists that "by 1940 the primary task of home economists and cookery instructors became to train women in consumption rather than production" (30). As cookbook authors aligned themselves with specific companies, hawking products ranging from electric stoves to canned goods, they also began to address the steady disappearance of servants from the middle-class home.

Working to convince middle-class housewives that a duty formerly assigned to domestic workers—cooking three meals a day, 365 days a year—was a fulfilling task, "cookbooks in the 1920s and 1930s aimed to give cooking an image overhaul and to reinvent it as an amusing and delightful occupation; [sic] an occupation suitable to the artistic, creative sensibilities of white middle-class ladies and not a laborious task best relegated to" the working classes (pp. 55–56). As Neuhaus points out, however, although their ideology centered around women's confinement to the kitchen, cookbooks also provided a form of escape for the middle-class housewife; cookbook sales rose during the Depression even though few "economical cookbooks" were published during this time—a fact indicating that at least some women bought cookery books to stir their imagination rather than for practical application. In other words, the same ideology that worked to contain the housewife in the kitchen likewise provided her with an escape from the budgetary constraints that made Depression-era cooking a daily struggle. By juxtaposing the "ideal" and the "real" Neuhaus foregrounds the provocative tension between two versions of domestic life, a tension that underscores a concurrent resistance and acquiescence to the prevailing domestic ideology.

Neuhaus' research repeatedly touches on the tensions between the real and the ideal in thought-provoking ways. She finds, for example, that while authors began to depict cooking as a "fun and creative task," they likewise made clear that it was a woman's duty—one upon which the family structure and even a stable society depended. Contrasting the ideal portrayed in cookery instruction with social reality, Neuhaus concludes that such instruction increasingly linked a family's well-being to the housewife's home cooking, in part to salve both the economic anxiety arising from the Depression and the domestic anxiety created by record numbers of women entering the workforce.

Such contextualization helps crystallize the importance of Neuhaus' research. So too does her observation that the more women stepped outside the home, the more powerfully cookery instruction worked to keep housewives safely contained in the home kitchen. In fact, *Manly Meals and Mom's Home Cooking* might include more such synthesis and analysis to shepherd the reader through the vast amount of material covered in each chapter and to tease out the broader implications of Neuhaus' research. The book might also benefit from tighter organization; at times, Neuhaus' argument circles back on itself, repeating material that has already been covered.

In her fourth chapter, Neuhaus examines 1920s and 1930s cookery instruction geared toward the male reader to show how it furthered the ideology of women as domestic creatures by depicting men as hobby cooks who "would never, ever cook like a woman" (p. 93). Nor should they want to, given the depiction of women's cooking as bland, fussy, and uninspired. Situating the message of men's cookery instruction within the broader historical context of the era, Neuhaus concludes that it insisted on the feminization of daily cooking in part because the traditional link between women and food preparation had been challenged by technology and the loss of hired help in the kitchen. As a result, she argues, authors "could not let a man enter the kitchen without scrupulously showing that male hobby cooking would not undermine the long-standing connection between women and food preparation and would not threaten masculine identity" (p. 76). This comment begs two questions. Precisely why did cookery instruction consistently maintain such a conservative stance that it "could not" let men cook for the family on a regular basis? And what did its authors stand to gain by keeping women in the kitchen?

Neuhaus devotes the middle section of her book to demonstrating how the trend toward domestic conservatism was heightened during World War II, when authors portrayed "cooking as the most important wartime employment of women" (p. 138) and as "an act of patriotism" (p. 117). They also began to employ rhetoric that echoed that of the Victorian era: women must create a restorative home environment that nurtured the family's well-being and prepared men both nutritionally and emotionally for public duty. After the war ended, cookbooks once again defined masculine and feminine appetites against one another. Just as it had in the 1920s and 1930s, instruction aimed at men often included what Neuhaus characterizes as "testosterone-infused directions" that drew largely on hunting and other sporting metaphors to describe cooking (p. 197). According to Neuhaus, male authors also repeatedly "insisted not only that men made inspired and excellent cooks, but that women prepared dull and tasteless daily meals" (p. 204).

While men, on one hand, were depicted as part-time gourmets, or, on the other, were given brief, and often humorous advice, on how to create "manly" dishes such as "Spanked Baby Dressing," women were given step-by-step instruction on "heating, combining, and augmenting canned and frozen foods" (p. 175). Some cookery instructors even felt compelled to tell their women readers precisely when to get dressed, light candles, announce dinner, and make coffee (p. 175).

According to Neuhaus, it was not until the late 1950s and the early 1960s that cookbooks and magazines began to openly address "the instability of the domestic ideal" (p. 257). Authors such as Peggy Bracken, whose *I Hate to Cook Book* became one of the nation's best-selling cookery titles, took part in a growing "resistance to the cult of domesticity" (p. 269). Despite this "resistance," however, Neuhaus concludes that "a powerful domestic cooking ideal" that places women in charge of daily meal preparation "continues to shape cookery instruction" to this day (p. 264). And, as her brief look at contemporary instruction suggests, "writers still characterize the man in the kitchen the same way their counterparts did" in the 1920s—as either a caveman who cooks outdoors over an open flame or as a hobby cook who, if the mood strikes, can concoct a few decidedly masculine dishes (p. 265).

Overall, *Manly Meals and Mom's Home Cooking* provides a thought-provoking examination of modern cookery instruction and its perpetuation of gender stereotypes. This last fact leaves me longing for a bibliography of Neuhaus's primary sources, although a lengthy essay covers the secondary ones.

Alice McLean
Sweet Briar College, VA
amclean@sbc.edu

TSUKIJI: THE FISH MARKET AT THE CENTER OF THE WORLD by Theodore C. Bestor (Berkeley, CA: University of California Press, 2004).

Theodore Bestor has written, as always, a detailed and thorough study of a fascinating and important institution. The book is not concerned strictly with food but it provides an excellent study of how food culture is structured by a variety of influences at different levels. The Tsukiji fish market is at the heart of Tokyo's old town in more than one way. It is a bastion of the traditional *shitamachi* (working-class) area of Tokyo and its residents' (many of whom are Tsukiji stalwarts) ability to maintain their traditional cultural view of life. Tsukiji is also the Wall Street of Japanese food consumption. It is here that the various seafoods, which, as Bestor points out, are at the heart of Japanese cuisine, are landed, sold and bought and, no less importantly, it is at Tsukiji that their prices are decided on for all of Japan, and thus, in essence, for much of the world.

In Chapter 1, Bestor provides his view of the relationship between culture and institutions, including economic institutions, and how these are expressed in the actual behaviors and products people engage in and with. Chapter 2 introduces Tsukiji as a phenomenon. Bestor traces the daily activities using a broad brush that he refines later.

He also delimits (if such a thing is possible) the spatial elements of Tsukiji market. These extend well beyond the geographical confines of the market. The spatial orientation, however, also determines the many stages upon which the actions take place with the selling of different types of seafood localized in specific areas of the market. Chapter 3 discusses the history of Tsukiji against the cultural and social history of Japan in the past two centuries. Chapter 4 is dedicated to the discussion of the main interest of Tsukiji: Japanese food culture. Bestor shows how the various influences—tradition, culinary choices from modernity, ecological reality and international law and relations—structure the nature of Japanese food and the sorts of food choices Japanese (and thus, to a lesser extent, the rest of their world) make.

In Chapter 5 Bestor veers to a discussion of the auctions—the nitty-gritty of the market, its real heart. If the nature of the market is seafood, its sinews and muscle are knowledge. Knowledge about consumer preferences (based upon tradition yet always mutating and changing), about prices, about how to go about selling and buying within Tsukiji's confines. And it is in the negotiation of knowledge that the buyers and sellers are actually structuring their interaction. The understanding of many institutions in Japanese society is predicated on understanding the nature of Japanese kinship. F.S.K. Hsu argued many years ago that the more traditional a Japanese institution is, the more likely it is to base its form on emulating Japanese kinship patterns. This is shown shows clearly in Chapter 6, where Bestor demonstrates how various forms of affiliation and alliance are dependent upon, and modeled by, traditional kinship patterns that, elsewhere in Japanese society, might be moribund.

Chapter 7 continues the sociological dimension by examining the wider implications and frameworks of social institutions, personal relationships, and coalitions within the institutional framework of Tsukiji.

In Chapter 8 Bestor returns to the cultural nature of the Tsukiji phenomenon as he also in a sense sounds its death knell: the market, driven by the price of land, is relocating from its current premises. How, and whether the balance of tradition, alliance, food, and salesmanship that is the hallmark of Tsukiji will be established again in the market's new premises, is debatable. The book ends with several necessary appendixes, notably a mini-chapter on how to get to Tsukiji, what to look (out) for, and a number of other "touristic" hints, and, perhaps more importantly, a glossary of useful terms.

Overall, Bestor has produced a remarkable book. I found Bestor's holistic description and interpretation to be in the best traditions of anthropological scholarship. However, therein lies a problem if one is interested particularly in the issue of food. Much of the thrust of the book is on the analysis of an important institution in Japanese society. Chapter 4, indeed, concentrates on the essence of the market (at least, from our point of view here): food. Bestor shows once again how various influences affect and have modified Japanese food choices and preferences. And, as Bestor himself notes, this is a *commercial* operation: the marketers are less concerned about the issue of *food* (though, as Japanese, as those engaged in the food business, and as Japanese who consider themselves traditional, this too is important) than about moving a commodity about.

We all know that the study of food does not begin or end with food itself. Inasmuch as food is the essential basis of all human activity, in a purely physical sense, it has implications that go well beyond its own nature. Bestor has managed to tease apart these different strands very well. That he approaches the issue from the point of view of looking at a social institution rather than at the nature of the food itself enhances, rather than detracts from, the description.

Overall, I would suggest (and indeed, Bestor himself says the same) that the reader be selective in reading this book. Some of the chapters, most notably 6 and 7 are likely to be tedious to the reader who is not either sociologically inclined or interested in the minutiae of Japanese society. Chapter 4 and the final chapter are worth reading in themselves because they shine additional light on the nature of Japanese food, contributing to the growing literature on the subject.

Michael Ashkenazi
Bonn International Centre for Conversion
ashkenazi@bicc.de

FOODS: EXPERIMENTAL PERSPECTIVES, FIFTH EDITION, and **EXPERIMENTAL FOODS: LABORATORY MANUAL, SIXTH EDITION** by Margaret McWilliams. Upper Saddle River, NJ: Prentice-Hall, Inc. 2004.

Foods: Experimental Perspectives and the accompanying laboratory manual are the newest editions of a widely used food science textbook and manual. The first edition of these books came out in the 1980s and they have been widely used as introductory food science texts ever since. While these books are grounded in the chemistry, physics, and biology of food science, they may be interesting and useful for food professionals in other fields.

In her introductory chapter, "The Dimensions of Food Studies," McWilliams addresses issues that confront the food industry today. Her discussion is based on the expectations and concerns of the food consumer, which is a good way to frame a debate of topical issues for an industry that shapes the food marketplace. The first section of this chapter has a succinct overview of organic and natural foods, phytochemicals, functional foods, biotechnology and genetically modified organisms, and the security of the national food supply.

The remainder of the text veers more directly into the vein of pure science. The second chapter, "The Research Process," is a concise look at the scientific research process. If my assumption that many of the readers of this journal are more versed in the qualitative types of research than quantitative types of research is correct, this look at the scientific method could prove interesting. McWilliams spends the chapter looking at the planning of experiments, how to approach the review of literature, and designing and evaluating experiments in food science. While the chapter is no substitute for a research methods class, as a short overview it could provide a good introduction to research, especially to undergraduates, who frequently do not get a good research grounding as part of the typical liberal arts education (at least at the universities I have been associated with).

Readers of this journal may be interested in the chapter on sensory evaluation. The author summarizes a good deal of the knowledge on the sensory characteristics of food, including recent research on the idea of *umami* as a fifth taste. Areas such as appearance, flavor, texture, and aroma are discussed using examples of how these attributes are measured scientifically and how they are evaluated from the food processing professional's perspective. How food is evaluated from the scientist's point of view gives some interesting insights into how we perceive foods as desirable based on these sensory characteristics.

While most of us would never think of evaluating our food with a shortometer, penetrometer, farinograph, masticometer, Warner-Bratzler shear, or Karl Fischer titrator, the book tells the budding food processor what all of these implements are and how to use them in order to measure certain characteristics of food via the use of instruments. Use of "objective evaluation devices" is widespread in the food-processing industry and it is interesting to see and learn about the tools they use to give us the consistent food product we have come to expect from them.

As the book continues into the sections on food processes and food products, the discussion takes place at an increasingly scientific level. At this point, having a background in science (or at least being able to remember some college chemistry and physics) would be helpful in gaining the most from the book. The section on processes begins with an explanation of the nature of water and the effects that water has on food products, both as an agent of food preparation and as a constituent of food products. It then continues with a discussion of the physical aspects of food preparation. Topics in this section include how food is affected by energy transfer—conduction, convection, and radiation—as well as issues such as solutions, emulsions, and change of state in food matter. These topics are the building blocks of basic cookery and a reader with a yen to know more about these topics could get a reasonable overview of these topics from this part of the book. The language and organization of the material in this section are not designed for casually dipping into the book, but rather as supporting material for the topics to come: the properties and actions of the physical food products.

In the sections on food products the author categorizes foods not as meat, vegetable and grain, or appetizer, entrée and dessert, but as carbohydrates, lipids, and proteins, giving the text a basic building block approach. It is in this section of the book that the reader uncomfortable with science may feel a bit intimidated, yet there are pieces in each of these sections that help the reader understand the principles behind common cookery. An example of this is the discussion of the caramelization of sugars and how this process creates pleasing flavors and textures in the foods we eat. This topic is not only approached from the molecular change point of view but gives practical advice on how to caramelize, how to stop the process, and what effect it has on various food products. Similar nuggets can be gleaned in the sections on lipids and proteins. For the amateur or professional cook or the food researcher there are many pieces of information that could be useful in a practical manner hidden among the long scientific explanations, micro-photographic images, and diagrams of food molecules.

The area of cooking that tends to engender the most questions is baking. Because baking is really more of a science than an art it has the greatest potential for problems for both the amateur and the professional. Bakers speak of formulas rather than recipes for good reason. Ingredients in baking perform multiple functions; for example, eggs give strength to a product, leaven it and moisturize it. When proportions are changed in a formula it changes the finished product in more than one way. This text has a comprehensive yet relatively accessible section on the ingredients and processes of baking. A cook wanting a brief overview of the role of ingredients in baking could find a good short discussion in this section.

Experimental Foods is obviously not an armchair read. It is a textbook and reads like one. What may recommend it to the professional in areas of food outside science is the way in which it can add a new dimension to the understanding of food products and processes. One of the strengths of this book is McWilliams' thorough definition of the terms that she uses in the text. Terms with which the reader is likely to be unfamiliar are highlighted in the text then defined in sidebars in the margin. This is an effective device for the reader as the flow of reading is interrupted as little as possible. There are a number of ingredient charts that could be quickly consulted for reference and a series of text boxes labeled "Food for Thought" give interesting asides on current topics such as carbohydrate avoidance, tofu, and the effect of sunlight on olive oil (it greatly speeds the rancidity of the product).

This book has been updated in a number of areas and appears to have successfully kept pace with advances in the food processing industry, but there are some graphics in the book that are in desperate need of an update. Some of the photographs appear to predate even the original edition of the book and an increase in the use of color would make the book more user friendly. Some graphics contributed by industry groups like the Wheat Flour Institute appear to be unchanged from the 1960s and seem quaint to this reviewer. I can't imagine that they would be useful in attracting young students to the world of food processing.

What readers must remember if they wish to use this book as a reference is that it is designed as a primer for the food-processing industry. While there is high quality technical information within its covers, it makes no apologies for a technical approach to food product preparation and usage. While the debate rages regarding topics such as the effects of hydrogenated oils on the body, this book approaches a topic like this as a food-processing issue, telling the future food processor how the processes work successfully in the food-processing arena, not a social issue, and how one avoids the use of these fats. Given this limitation and others noted previously, this book could be a useful addition to the bookshelf of the non-science food professional.

Jeffrey Miller
Colorado State University
jmiller@cahs.colostate.edu

AGRARIAN DREAMS: THE PARADOX OF ORGANIC FARMING IN CALIFORNIA by Julie Guthman (Berkeley, CA: University of California Press, 2004).

If midway twixt plate and lip your taste anticipation of a succulent forkful of perfectly dressed organic baby greens causes you to dream of the idyllic organic small-farm lifestyle personified by those back-to-the-land "grounded" and "ecologically sound" organic farm pioneers in California, stop your daydream immediately. Most likely your tender greens are the products of a large capitalistic factory farm designed specifically to provide greens to high-income consumers all over America, having been produced at the lowest possible price using low-wage illegal and green-card labor and by adhering only to the letter of the law in utilizing organic principles to meet minimum requirements for labeling. This process, explains author Julie Guthman, exemplifies the agricultural organic-food movement in California, which grew out of standard factory-farming agronomy methods, financial structures, and agricultural histories and that ultimately privileges expansion of large conventional growers over support of the idealistic adherents of the sustainable and ecologically sound small-family-farm model which comes to mind when the word "organic" is used in reference to food.

Everyone interested in food policy should read this book, especially if interested in how public policy, agricultural financial structures, consumer demand, and media-and-marketing concepts can dictate the processes of food production. Dr Guthman neatly outlines how the rosy ideal of the sustainable agriculture movement—the land-owning yeoman farmer with a smallholding worked solely by family labor—is a myth borne from American cultural models of family structure and function, agricultural/financial independence, and unrealistic projections of ecological best practices. She argues that the agricultural processes of organic farming are often the same as those of conventional farming, that the elements which determine developmental processes and outcomes are a continuum of standard agricultural developments in California, and that these realities and processes are not represented by the ideology that surrounds the concept of organic agriculture. In short, the trademarked icon of the ideal farm and barn glimpsed on the label of that bottle of Walnut Acres organic spaghetti sauce may be merely a marketing image designed to evoke the invented-nostalgia fantasy of a purified, sustainable, equitable and healthy "agrarian dream" lifestyle. The farm that produced the tomato within is more likely to be a rented section of a larger conventional holding, worked by immigrant migrant labor paid less than minimum wage, organic in name only due to the absence of industrial-agricultural inputs rather than careful soil or land management, and designed to provide a small cushion of profit in a thoroughly industrialized and bitterly competitive vegetable market which rewards risk-taking spasmodically.

Her methods are qualitative and quantitative, combining agricultural land-use data with histories of Californian agricultural patterns, policy developments and financing and tying it all together with ethnographic interviews of organic farmers. Of particular importance is her examination of how use patterns have been dictated by the financial values of specific land holdings, and how these processes then fold into the development of specific kinds of agricultural practices and outcomes. She contrasts the health-seeking valorization of the organic food "lifestyle" ideal, made popular by demand for gourmet foods and arising out of the high-end alternative food markets of the San Francisco and Santa Cruz metropolitan areas, with the realities of a Californian agricultural history marked by land speculation and large landholder farming strategies—indeed one that never sustained the agrarian-populist ideal of the yeoman-farmer owner-producer smallholding. Indeed, the very agencies that then arose to create and certify reputable organic products have served primarily to allow larger landholders to capture a market viewed as hugely lucrative rather than an element in an ecologically sustainable world. As such, the goals of the organic producer are very different from those of the organics consumer, and this study chronicles the rise of industrial organics while simultaneously shredding the fantasies of the "sustainable agriculture" movement.

Guthman begins with an outline and history of the Agrarian Ideal, paying particular attention to how discourses of citizenship premised the yeoman farmer as the model American and how this trope then folded into the political-economic ideals of civic and personal renewal popular in the 1960s and 1970s and which led to the countercultural food movement. Chapters 2 and 3 examine the various histories of organic farming—the routes by which individual farmers (and eventually farm corporations) came to adopt and support organic farming processes. As one would expect, this trajectory often begins with smallholding ideals and alternative methods and as success builds and the market dictates increased volumes, morphs into agro-industrial conglomerates, which alter methods to meet marketplace needs and increase profit margins. The dictum to "grow large or fail" has forced most medium-sized farms to either adopt more competitive value-added production methods or to merge with larger concerns to survive financing needs, while only smaller direct-market oriented organic truck farms can survive utilizing the full roster of organic farming principles, largely because of decreased outreach costs due to grower-to-client marketing structures such as CSAs (Community-Supported

Agriculture) and farmers markets. In Chapters 4 and 5, Guthman outlines the agricultural history of California, capably demonstrating how financial structures and land costs have dictated farm processes. Of particular importance is the very high cost of agricultural land, which often makes farm startup reliant on land rental and farmers unwilling to invest in organic improvements in fear that landlords may raise rents to reflect the increased values of organic-certified farm land. She demonstrates that in California agricultural industrialization and development follows a pattern of intensification, appropriation, and valorization and that this applies to organic as well as conventional processes—so much so that organic food production has become an element of the conventional farming strategy since it allows entrepreneurial manipulation of the three principles—but always within a purely capitalistic model.

In Chapter 5 Guthman constructs a geographic profile of the California regions to illusstrate that in each area, organic farmers constructed food production practices and strategies by building upon already-developed structures of farm economics, land management, and social systems:

> In short, once growers began to convert to organic production, it simply was not or could not be inserted into the landscape without confronting existing patterns. In effect, it has been layered ... upon existing California agriculture and the social relations they embody, making some adjustments within but rarely transforming structures and practices. This occurs because growers who convert to organic production inherit what are already well-defined crop specializations as well as the entire ensemble of land tenure, marketing arrangements, labor organization, technical support, and so forth, that evolve around these specializations. Yet, the easy replication of commodity specializations is not the only cause. After all, growers can always change what they grow, and many do. The more fundamental problem is that regional land values have been capitalized on the basis of these specializations, constraining what can be grown and by what methods. It is in this way that past regional development so strongly shapes organic futures. (Guthman 2004: 108)

This neatly sums up the thesis of the book, demonstrating both the strengths and weaknesses of the organic model utilized in California.

Guthman ends her analysis with an outline of the various processes and histories that created the present organic certification structure, emphasizing that the process has been developed by, and remains in the control of, agencies that safeguard the interests of the larger agricultural producers. As such, certification has become a labeling exercise, which can be virtually meaningless when applied to concepts of food safety, land sustainability, or ecological management. But then again, as she makes clear, it was never designed to meet the needs of consumers or agricultural reformers; certification has always been a means to provide value to products in order that their market price is increased. Her summation (Chapter 8) reminds us that as currently practiced, organic agriculture in California does not "provide a trenchant alternative to the interwoven mechanisms that simultaneously bring hunger and surplus, waste and danger, and wealth and poverty in the ways food is grown, processed, and traded" (Guthman 2004: 22). In particular

> herein lies the paradox of organic farming in California. Like all growers, organic farmers must make payments to land. Since past rounds of

intensification and innovation have been capitalized into land values, current land values reflect the social and ecological exploitations that produced profitability in each of those rounds. Indeed, since much land in California has been capitalized on the basis of intensive horticultural production, it has been made too costly for alternative sorts of production systems. Unless growers find some other subsidy to land, they must replicate such exploitation to remain financially viable. (Guthman 2004: 178)

In short, land must be subsidized—via direct land gifts (tax-free or reduced-tax inheritance based on farm preservation), foundation capital inputs, and/or publicly-supported tax easements in order to be able to support the risk and lower yields of fully integrated organic production.

Yet Guthman also provides hope by outlining how the processes of farm management might be altered to make land and farm preservation more attentive to organic entrepreneurial activities. She suggests that direct marketing can play an essential role in reducing farm inputs and thereby raising farm profits, and that further public support of CSA structures may benefit many small and mid-sized truck farmers who utilize fully organic and ecological practices. She also points out the need to examine wage structures in relation to organic output costs, and in particular to call upon consumers to support fair-wage "not-so-cheap" foods. Ultimately, she illustrates that food is a commodity and that we must examine the structures and processes of commodification accurately, fairly, and without unrealistic expectations in order to move toward more sustainable, equitable, and ecologically sound agricultural practices.

As stated earlier, this is a must-read book for all students and practitioners of food production and policy. However, Guthman has done her own work and inspired thesis a disservice by blending what seem to be three conceptually interlinked studies into a single thematic construction. First, there is the history of agriculture and organic certification, combined with the development of organic farming within the regional and economic structures that simultaneously shape and determine form, function, and process. Second, buried within this text are intriguing clues to the economic and ecological strategies of individual farmers that, if expanded, would provide invaluable knowledge of how conventional agriculture might be reformatted successfully to allow expansion of organics into more areas of American agriculture. Guthman used semi-structured techniques to interview over 150 organic growers, both large and small, to understand how they made and implemented decisions about shifting to organic, process adoption, goals, outcome potentials, and profit structures. Notes within the overall text hint at intriguing and very adaptive strategies for maximizing profit while minimizing farm risk. And finally, she has constructed a rhetorical paper tiger that could be augmented to better explore and understand the conceptual constructions which govern the split between producer realities and consumer ideologies of food production. This latter theme could simply be boiled down to a simplistic "the organic food myth is all hype and media puff", but that would ill serve producers and consumers. Ultimately, if consumers understood the origins and manifestations of their organic mythologies they could prove to be far better and far more critical consumers—a process that would create opportunities for true agricultural reform.

Janet Chrzan
University of Pennsylvania
jdamkrog@sas.upenn.edu

Contributors ::

HELENE BREMBECK is Associate Professor at the Department of Ethnology, and research leader at Center for Consumer Science, Göteborg University, Box 600, SE-405 30 Göteborg, Sweden (helene.brembeck@cfk.gu.se). She has led several research projects concerning children, childhood, parenthood and consumption, including food and eating, and published several articles and books within this field, such as Det konsumerande barnet (*The Consuming Child*) (2001). She is the editor of *Elusive Consumption* together with Karin M. Ekström (Berg, 2004), and *Beyond the Competent Child* together with Barbro Johansson and Jan Kampmann (Roskilde University Press, 2004). Currently she is the leader of the research project *Commercial Cultures in an Ethnological and Economical Perspective*. Her own subproject concerns parents and children at McDonald's, and it is presented in this article. She is also working on a project on the baby boomers and food.

CAROLE COUNIHAN is Professor of Anthropology at Millersville University in Pennsylvania, Millersville, PA 17551, USA (carole.counihan@millersville.edu). She is co-editor in chief of *Food and Foodways* and has been pursuing the ethnographic study of food and culture for two decades. She has authored and edited several books including *Food and Culture: A Reader* (with Penny Van Esterik, Routledge 1997), *The Anthropology of Food and Body* (Routledge 1999), *Food in the USA: A Reader* (Routledge 2002), and *Around the Tuscan Table: Food, Family and Gender in Twentieth Century Florence* (Routledge 2004). Her next project is to write a book based on food-centered life histories with *Mexicanas* in the San Luis Valley of Colorado.

KELLY DONATI is an MA graduate from the gastronomy program at the University of Adelaide in Australia (kdonati@internode.on.net). She has also completed an MA in critical theory and cultural studies at Monash University. Her research interests include gastronomy, the politics of food, feminist philosophy, literary criticism and psychoanalytic theory. Kelly is currently working as a researcher at the Globalism Institute RMIT.

JAMES E. MCWILLIAMS is an Assistant Professor of History at Texas State University, 601 University Drive, San Marcos, TX 78666, USA (jm71@txstate.edu). His book, titled *A Revolution in Eating: How the Quest for Food Shaped America* (Columbia University Press) came out in July 2005.

LUANNE ROTH is an instructor in the English Department at the University of Missouri, Columbia, MO 65201, USA (RothL@missouri.edu), where she teaches courses in American folklore, particularly food and culture, folk art and material culture, and family folklore. She is also managing editor of the *Journal of American Folklore*. Having earned her MA in folklore and mythology from UCLA, she is completing her PhD in English. She has published several articles on the folklore of Grateful Dead fans and has a book-length work forthcoming, *Shakedown Street: The Art of Deadheads* (University Press of Mississippi). Her current research involves exploring the explosion of "ethnic" restaurants in the West as well as examining disruptive and subversive representations of family meals in literature, film, and in real life.

KYLA WAZANA TOMPKINS is an Assistant Professor of English and Women's Studies at Pomona College, Claremont, CA 91711, USA (Kyla.Tomkins@pomona.edu). She is a former restaurant critic and food writer and has been writing about and studying food for over a decade. She is presently working on a book about food and racial formation in the nineteenth-century US titled: *Stomaching Difference: Race, Food and the Body Politic in the Nineteenth-Century United States*.

ASHBY WALKER is a PhD candidate in the Department of Sociology at Emory University, Tarbutton Hall, Atlanta, GA 30322, USA (afarmer@emory.edu). Ashby's areas of focus include social psychology, culture and media. Her dissertation research examines the symbolic representation of food and gender in magazine advertisements throughout the past century. Ashby teaches the Sociology of Food and Eating.

Notes for Contributors : :

Food, Culture & Society is published by the Association for the Study of Food and Society (ASFS). ASFS is a multidisciplinary international organization dedicated to exploring the complex relationships among food, culture, and society. Its members approach the study of food from numerous disciplines in the humanities, social sciences, and sciences, as well as in the world of food beyond the academy. Striving to represent the highest standards of research and scholarship in all aspects of food studies, we encourage vigorous debate on a wide range of topics and problems, such as:

   cross-cultural perspectives on eating behaviors
   gender and the food system
   the food voice
   recipes, cookbooks, and menus as texts
   philosophical and religious perspectives on food and the body
   social construction of culinary practices, beliefs, and traditions
   politics of the family meal
   dietary transitions
   psychological, cultural, and social determinants of taste
   methodological issues in food studies
   malnutrition, hunger, and food security
   commodity chain and foodshed analysis
   food in fiction, film, and art
   comparative food history
   social and cultural dimensions of food technologies
   political economy of the global food system
   food studies pedagogy
   plus original reviews of relevant books, films, videos, and exhibitions

Authors do not have to be members of ASFS to submit articles. Manuscripts will be subject to a blind peer review by members of the FCS Board of Editors and ad hoc reviewers. If accepted for publication in this journal, the author(s) must agree not to publish it elsewhere in the same form, in English or any other language, without the written consent of the editor. Copyright will be held by ASFS.

We prefer that contributors send their paper electronically via email to the editor, Warren Belasco: belasco@umbc.edu. Articles that discuss the teaching of food studies should be sent to John Deutsch: jdeutsch@kingsborough.edu. The e-mail itself will serve as the submission letter and should indicate that the paper has not been published elsewhere, in whole or in part, and that it has not been submitted simultaneously for publication elsewhere.

Authors are strongly encouraged to submit manuscripts in English. MS Word is the preferred software program. Each of the following sections should begin on a new page: title page, abstract (150 words or less), bio (150 words), text, acknowledgments, notes and references, illustration legends, each illustration, each table. Manuscripts should be double spaced, use Times New Roman 12-point font, with 1 inch margins, and be created on 8½ × 11 inch letter (or A4) size pages. Pages should be numbered at the center bottom.

References and notes must conform to a known citation style – usually Chicago (historical/literary) or APA (social science). For specifics, please consult Kate L. Turabian, *A Manual for Writers of Term Papers, Theses, and Dissertations* (latest edn).

Illustrations submitted should be clean originals or digital files. Digital files are recommended for highest quality reproduction and should follow these guidelines:

- 300 dpi or higher
- sized to fit on a journal page
- submitted as separate electronic files (e.g. TIFF or JPG files), not embedded in text files

Color illustrations will be considered for publication only if the author agrees to pay the full cost of their printing and publication.

Authors are responsible for obtaining permission to reproduce copyrighted material.

Final revisions of accepted manuscripts should be submitted in MS Word via email or disk to the *FCS* editor. The name of electronic files should be clearly labeled. Short biographies (150 words) of all authors are required for accepted manuscripts and should include name, position, department, institution, plus ground mail and e-mail addresses. *FCS* reserves the right to make minor stylistic changes that, in the opinion of the editor, do not change the meaning of the article or the views of the author.

The first-named author will receive one copy of the issue in which his/her article appears and 25 free offprints. Additional copies and offprints can be purchased on request.

Address all correspondence to the FCS editor: Warren Belasco, American Studies Department, University of Maryland Baltimore County, Baltimore, MD 21250, USA (e-mail: belasco@umbc.edu)

More information about ASFS may be found at: http://food-culture.org/